Doing Action Research
In Your Own Organization

Doing Action Research
In Your Own Organization

Second Edition

David Coghlan
Teresa Brannick

Los Angeles • London • New Delhi • Singapore

First published 2005
Reprinted 2005, 2006, 2007 (twice), 2008

SAGE Publications Ltd
1 Oliver's Yard
55 City Road
London EC1Y 1SP

SAGE Publications Inc
2455 Teller Road
Thousand Oaks, California 91320

SAGE Publications India Pvt Ltd
B 1/I 1 Mohan Cooperative Industrial Area
Mathura Road, New Delhi 110 044
India

SAGE Publications Asia-Pacific Pte Ltd
33 Pekin Street #02-01
Far East Square
Singapore 048763

British Library Cataloguing in Publication data

A catalogue record for this book is available from the British Library

ISBN 978-1-4129-0246-5
ISBN 978-1-4129-0247-2 (pbk)

Library of Congress Control Number 2004096489

Typeset by M Rules
Printed in Great Britain by The Cromwell Press Ltd, Trowbridge, Wiltshire

Contents

About the Authors

DAVID COGHLAN is a member of the faculty of the School of Business Studies, University of Dublin, Trinity College, Dublin, Ireland where he teaches organization development and action research and participates actively in both communities internationally. He has an MSc in management science from Manchester University (UK), an SM in management from MIT's Sloan School of Management, a PhD from the National University of Ireland and an MA from the University of Dublin. He is co-author of *The Dynamics of Organizational Levels* in the Addison-Wesley OD series (1994), *Changing Healthcare Organisations* (Blackhall, 2003) and co-editor of *Managers Learning in Action* (Routledge, 2004), a collection of research accounts of managers who engaged in action research in their own organizations. He is a member of the editorial advisory board of *Action Research*.

TERESA BRANNICK is a lecturer in the business research programme at the Michael Smurfit Graduate School of Business at University College, Dublin, Ireland. Her undergraduate degree is in mathematics, her masters in sociology and her PhD in marketing research. She has been a practising researcher for over twenty years and has published over thirty research papers in such diverse fields as epidemiology, public policy, industrial relations and marketing. She is the editor of the *Irish Journal of Management*. She is co-editor of *Business Research Methods: Theories, Techniques and Sources* (Oak Tree Press: Dublin, 1997). She conducts seminars on research methods and on researching your own organization.

Preface

Researching your own organization, and more particularly through an action research approach, is a neglected subject in the research literature. Typically, action research is presented in terms of situations where an action researcher, external to an organization, enters the organization in some sort of temporary facilitative role, works with the members of the organization for the duration of the project and then leaves. What is less common is a presentation of action research from within organizations, conducted by action researchers who are permanent and full members of the organization. When we originally embarked on the first edition of this book, we used every opportunity we could to inquire among colleagues, both at home and abroad, at conferences and by e-mail, what they knew to have been written on the topic. The typical response was to confirm the paucity of publication on the subject, both theory and case material, and to encourage us to fill this gap. At the same time, everyone we consulted acknowledged that the practice of doing action research in and on your own organization was very common.

In the few years since the publication of the first edition, the practice of insider action research has burgeoned. The consolidation of doctoral action research in universities around the world has contributed considerably to the legitimization of insider action research by practitioners in all sectors of organizational life – for example, business, healthcare, nursing, education, social and community work.

At the same time, our understanding and conceptualization of insider action research has developed. In his notion of 'innovation action research', Kaplan (1998) presents an action research cycle of: observing and documenting practice; teaching and speaking about it; writing articles and books; implementing the concept; and moving to advanced implementation. After several years of observing and documenting practice, teaching and speaking about it, writing articles and books, thereby implementing the concept, we ourselves see this revised edition as advanced implementation. The theory and practice of doing action research in your own organization or insider action research, as it is also called, has advanced. In this edition, after several years of an innovation cycle we are more confident of our ground and of the contribution this book has to make.

What is action research? As the name suggests, action research is an approach to research which aims at both taking action and creating knowledge or theory about that action. The outcomes are both an action and a research outcome, unlike traditional research approaches which aim at creating knowledge only. Action research works through a cyclical process of consciously and deliberately: (a) planning; (b) taking action; (c) evaluating the action, leading to further planning and so on. The second dimension of action research is that it is collaborative, in that the members of the system which is being studied participate actively in the cyclical process. This contrasts with traditional research where members are objects of the study. Action research is a generic term that covers many forms of action-oriented research, which may be confusing to any prospective researcher. At the same time, the array of approaches indicates diversity in theory and practice among action researchers and provides a wide choice for potential action researchers as to what might be appropriate for their research.

Action research is appropriate when the research topic is an unfolding series of actions over time in a given group, community or organization, and the members wish to study their own action in order to change or improve the working of some aspects of the system, and study the process in order to learn from it. Hence action research is akin to experiential learning and reflective practice.

Doing research in one's own organization means that a member of an organization undertakes an explicit research role in addition to the normal functional role which that member holds in the organization. Therefore, the researcher has to balance the membership role he or she holds and hopes to continue to hold with the additional role of inquiry and research. Doing action research means being engaged in a more rigorous series of diagnosing situations, planning and taking action and evaluating than is perhaps the norm.

There are many issues to be considered for those embarking on research in their own organization or part thereof. From the perspective of individuals who are seeking to do the research in order to achieve academic certification, there are issues pertaining to their academic directors and those pertaining to their organizational superiors. There are issues of gaining access and receiving permission, and building and maintaining support from peers and relevant subsystems within the organization. There are issues of selecting a research question and area for study. In such a case, student-researchers, in effect, take on an additional role to their conventional organizational one, that of active agent of inquiry. This multiple role identity both complicates and focuses the research project. There are issues around how to attain some sense of objectivity and move beyond a personal perspective by testing assumptions and interpretations. There are the uses of appropriate frameworks for viewing and understanding the data. There are questions about how to write up such a research project, give feedback to one's superiors and peers, and disseminate the research to the wider community. Handling interpretations or outcomes which would be perceived negatively by the organization is a particularly sensitive issue.

Who does action research in their own organization? A common context for such research is one where an individual employee undertakes research as part of an academic programme in order to fulfil requirements for academic certification (Gosling and Ashton, 1994; Zuber-Skerritt and Perry, 1994). In this instance the individual initiates the research agenda and attempts to negotiate a research project which will meet both his or her own and the organization's needs. This occurs in full-time and part-time programmes, at doctorate, masters, undergraduate and diploma levels and in business, healthcare, government, education, social work and third sector organizations. Some research projects may be integrally linked to inquiry into the processes of problem resolution; others may take a broader, more comprehensive and diagnostic perspective. At the same time, selection of a research topic from one's own organization is typically attached to an expectation or contract that the research will make a useful contribution to the organization.

Readership

This book is addressed to the reader who is in this dual role of simultaneously holding an organizational functional role which is linked to a career path and ongoing membership of the organization, and a more temporary researcher role for the duration of the research project. While this may imply a distinction between research and ordinary life, we do not intend such a distinction. Our aim is to provide a book which is useful for those who select an action research role in their own organization for a temporary period, and for those in academic institutions who supervise such research.

There are many books that address the theory and practice of action research (Argyris, et al., 1985; Schein, 1987; Elliot, 1991; Whyte, 1991; Greenwood and Levin, 1998; Stringer, 1999; Gummesson, 2000; Reason and Bradbury, 2001; Adler et al., 2004). We do not intend retracing what is well presented in these works, particularly with regard to epistemological issues, the history of action research and detailed formats of research interventions. Indeed we recommend that this book be used in conjunction with such works as: Hart and Bond (1995), Greenwood and Levin (1998), Stringer (1999), Gummesson (2000), Reason and Bradbury (2001) and Adler et al. (2004).

Plan of the book

The book is divided into three parts. Part I, Foundations, introduces and explores foundational material on action research. Chapter 1 provides a description of action research. Chapter 2 describes the action research cycle. Chapter 3 focuses on how the action researcher learns in action.

Part II, Issues and Challenges in Researching Your Own Organization, deals with issues of doing action research in your own organization. Chapter 4 explores in outline four different forms which insider research can take, depending on the system's and your own explicit commitment to learning in action. Chapter 5 discusses how your preunderstanding and taking on the researcher role in addition to your organizational roles need attention. Chapter 6 examines the important role of managing organizational politics and of managing ethics. Chapter 7 focuses on framing and selecting a project.

Part III, Implementation, deals with issues of putting your action research project into action. Chapter 8 outlines the actual process of implementing the action research project. Chapter 9 shows how implementation involves working with individuals, teams and across groups. Chapter 10 introduces some frameworks for diagnosing organizations and applying theory. Chapter 11 provides some hints on writing an action research dissertation.

David Coghlan
Teresa Brannick
Dublin

Acknowledgements

We are grateful to those action research colleagues and friends who read the first edition and provided valuable support, feedback and ideas for the revision: Chris Argyris, Mary Casey, Allan Church, Paul Coughlan, Evert Gummesson, Bruce Hanson, Claus Jacobs, Jim Ludema, Eilish McAuliffe, Patrick Nolan, Terry Orr, Mike Pedler, Peter Reason, Rami Shani, Bill Torbert and Graham Williamson.

We are very grateful for the feedback from the many groups who used the first edition in courses and seminars. We acknowledge the feedback from successive cohorts of the Masters in Management Practice programme at the Irish Management Institute-University of Dublin, the Masters in Health Service Management at the University of Dublin and the MBA at the Smurfit Graduate School of Business, University College, Dublin, as they contributed to refining some of the frameworks as they struggled through their own insider action research projects. We also received helpful comments through working with doctoral groups at Benedictine University in the USA, Cranfield University in the UK and the FENIX programme in Stockholm School of Economics. Doctoral groups at Colorado Technical University and Teachers' College, Columbia University provided specific feedback for this revision.

Several individuals who undertook action research in their own organizations – Mary Casey, Rosa Colon, Pip Ferguson, Sheelagh Kelly, Dan Kowalski and Rita Kowalski – provided particular feedback from their own experience.

Paula Roberts took our handwritten diagrams and skilfully turned them into graphics. We acknowledge the invaluable help and support of the Sage editorial and production teams, especially Patrick Brindle and Vanessa Harwood.

Part I
Foundations

1

Understanding Action Research

In this chapter we outline the foundations of action research through describing its core tenets and illustrating how it has become a generic term for a wide array of related approaches.

What is action research?

In the words of Reason and Bradbury, 'action research is a participatory, democratic process concerned with developing practical knowing in the pursuit of worthwhile human purposes, grounded in a participatory worldview' (2001: 1). This working definition provides a flavour of the broad scope and intent of action research with the ultimate aim of 'the flourishing of the individual person and their communities'. Shani and Pasmore provide a more restricted definition:

> Action research may be defined as an emergent inquiry process in which applied behavioural science knowledge is integrated with existing organizational knowledge and applied to solve real organizational problems. It is simultaneously concerned with bringing about change in organizations, in developing self-help competencies in organizational members and adding to scientific knowledge. Finally, it is an evolving process that is undertaken in a spirit of collaboration and co-inquiry. (Shani and Pasmore, 1985: 439)

Given the context of this book, where we expect readers to be working on action research projects in their own organizations, we are working more from Shani and Pasmore's definition than Reason and Bradbury's.

Several broad characteristics define action research:

- research *in* action, rather than research *about* action;
- a collaborative democratic partnership;

- concurrent with action;
- a sequence of events and an approach to problem solving.

We will discuss each in turn.

First, action research focuses on research *in* action, rather than research *about* action. The central idea is that AR uses a scientific approach to study the resolution of important social or organizational issues together with those who experience these issues directly. Action research works through a cyclical four-step process of consciously and deliberately: planning; taking action; evaluating the action; leading to further planning, and so on.

Second, AR is a collaborative, democratic partnership. Members of the system which is being studied participate actively in the cyclical process outlined above. Such participation contrasts with traditional research where members of the system are subjects or objects of the study. An important qualitative element of action research is how people are drawn into the processes of inquiry and action and how they participate and collaborate.

Third, AR is research concurrent with action. The goal is to make that action more effective while simultaneously building up a body of scientific knowledge.

Finally, AR is both a sequence of events and an approach to problem solving. As a sequence of events, it comprises iterative cycles of gathering data, feeding it back to those concerned, analysing the data, planning action, taking action and evaluating, leading to further data gathering and so on. As an approach to problem solving, it is an application of the scientific method of fact-finding and experimentation to practical problems requiring action solutions and involving the collaboration and co-operation of the action researchers and members of the organizational system. The desired outcomes of the action research approach are not just solutions to the immediate problems but are important learning from outcomes both intended and unintended, and a contribution to scientific knowledge and theory.

Research paradigms and action research

How is action research scientific? Many writers have articulated the ontological and epistemological foundations of action research and contrasted them with those of the scientific method associated with positivistic philosophy (Susman and Evered, 1978; Riordan, 1995; Eden and Huxham, 1996; Greenwood and Levin, 1998, Gummesson, 2000; Reason and Torbert, 2001). It is not our intention to retrace those arguments here but instead we will give a brief general overview of the three main traditions, positivism, hermeneutics and critical realism (see Table 1.1).

TABLE 1.1 **RESEARCH PARADIGMS AND ACTION RESEARCH**

Philosophical foundations	Positivism	Hermeneutic and postmodernism	Critical realism and action research
Ontology	Objectivist	Subjectivist	Objectivist
Epistemology	Objectivist	Subjectivist	Subjectivist
Theory	Generalizable	Particular	Particular
Reflexivity	Methodological	Hyper	Epistemic
Role of researcher	Distanced from data	Close to data	Close to data

The philosophy of science has produced useful principles relating to epistemology and ontology which include some basic assumptions that constitute the philosophical underpinnings of warranted knowledge or theory. This in turn enables us to understand science and differing forms of explanation. Epistemology (the grounds for knowledge) and ontology (the nature of the world) can be assessed along a fairly arbitrary continuum moving from an objectivist (realist) to a subjectivist (relativist) perspective. Researchers' epistemological and ontological perspectives legitimate their own distinctive way of doing research and determine what they consider as a valid, legitimate contribution to knowledge or theory irrespective of whether we called it development, confirmation, validation, creation, building or generation (Peter and Olsen, 1983). An objectivist view of epistemology accepts the possibility of a theory-neutral language, in other words it is possible to access the external world objectively. A subjectivist view denies the possibility of a theory-neutral language. An objectivist view of ontology assumes that social and natural reality have an independent existence prior to human cognition whereas a subjectivist ontology assumes that what we take as reality is an output of human cognitive process (Johnson and Duberley, 2000). Different epistemological and ontological approaches encourage different kinds of reflexivity. Even though reflexivity is not a new concept to the social sciences its importance has only come to the fore in recent times (Bourdieu, 1990).

Reflexivity is the social sciences concept used to explore and deal with the relationship between the researcher and the object of research. Reflection means thinking about the conditions for what one is doing, investigating the way in which the theoretical, cultural and political context of individual and intellectual involvement affects interaction with whatever is being researched, often in ways difficult to become conscious of (Alvesson and Skoldberg, 2000).

Systematic reflexivity is the constant analysis of one's own theoretical and methodological presuppositions which helps with retaining an awareness of the importance of other people's definitions and understandings of theirs (Lynch, 1999). Johnson and Duberley (2000) subdivide systematic reflexivity into two forms, epistemic and methodological. Epistemic reflexivity focuses on the researcher's belief system and is the process for analysing and challenging our meta-theoretical assumptions. Methodological reflexivity is concerned with the monitoring of our behavioural impact upon the research setting as a result of carrying out the research. This requires us to follow the research procedure and protocols identified and demanded by the different research traditions.

The dominant approach or paradigm in management and organizational studies has been positivism and its successors (explanation, hypothetico-deductive, multi-method eclecticism). These approaches are defined primarily by their view that an external reality exists and that an independent value-free researcher can examine this reality. In other words they adhere to an objectivist (realist) ontology and an objectivist epistemology. Positivists adopt a method-ological approach towards reflexivity and concentrate on improving methods and their application (Johnson and Duberley, 2000). The aim of positivist sci-ence is the creation of generalizable knowledge or covering laws. In positivist science findings are validated by logic, measurement and the consistency achieved by the consistency of prediction and control. The positivist scientist's relationship to the setting is one of neutrality and detachment.

The hermeneutic tradition, the other main approach (sometimes referred to as phenomenology, constructivist, interpretivist, postmodern interpretivism rel-ativist approach), argues that there is no objective or single knowable external reality, and that the researcher is an integral part of the research process, not sep-arate from it. This distinction is based on the subject–object dichotomy. This ontological 'subjective versus objective' dimension concerns the assumptions social theories make about the nature of the social world. This approach follows a subjectivist (relativist) ontology and epistemology. Inquiry is inherently value-laden. Postmodernism tends to adopt a hyper-reflexivity which focuses on reflexive deconstruction of own practice. Hermeneutic inquiry is directed towards the development of particular or idiographic knowledge. Nothing can be measured without changing it and this insider close to the data perspective provides valid rich and deep data.

The third approach identified by Johnson and Duberley is critical realism incorporating pragmatic critical realism and aligns with our concept and under-standing of action research. This approach follows a subjectivist epistemology similar to the hermeneutic tradition but an objectivist ontology like the posi-tivists. This approach concentrates on epistemic reflexivity which looks at exposing interests and enabling emancipation through self-reflexivity. Reflexivity is not a neutral process and is in itself socially and historically conditioned. If reflexivity is to facilitate change it needs to be guided by principles of democratic engagement and a commitment to change. Reflective knowledge has to do with normative states in social, economic and political realms. It concerns a vision of what ought to be, what is right and what is wrong and arises through the process of consciousness-raising and conscientization (Reason and Bradbury, 2001).

Action research focuses on knowledge in action. Accordingly, the knowledge created through action research is particular, situational and out of praxis. In action research the data are contextually embedded and interpreted. In action research, the basis for validation is the conscious and deliberate enactment of the action research cycle. The action researcher is immersed in the research setting.

Action research approaches are radical to the extent that they advocate replacement of existing forms of social organization. Action research challenges normal science in several action-oriented ways. Sharing the power of knowledge production with the researched subverts the normal practice of knowledge and policy development as being the primary domain of researchers and policy-makers. Action researchers work on the epistemological assumption that the purpose of academic research and discourse is not just to describe, understand and explain the world but also to change it (Reason and Torbert, 2001). The issue is not so much the form of the knowledge produced or the methodology employed to gather data/evidence but who decides the research agenda in the first place and who benefits directly from it.

In short, the contrast of roles is between that of detached observer in positivist science and of an actor and agent of change in action research (Evered and Louis, 1981). Weisbord (1988) explores the images of taking photographs and making films in relation to organization development. He describes taking photographs as freezing a moment in time and arranging key factors in a conceptual framework. No photograph takes in the whole of reality; it only takes in what is in the frame. Photographers decide what is to be in the frame and they manipulate the setting to include and exclude desirable and undesirable features. Making films is an engagement in patterns of activity and relationships by multiple actors who are moving and interacting over a period of time. It is increasingly common to find actors directing their own films. In these cases, actor-directors engage in their acting role in costume and then return to behind the camera in order to study the take, critique it and make decisions about proceeding to the next take. We find this image of making films and the action researcher as an actor-director pertinent and useful for thinking about doing action research. As Riordan expresses it, action research is:

a kind of approach to studying social reality without separating (while distinguishing) fact from value; they require a practitioner of science who is not only
an engaged participant, but also incorporates the perspective of the critical
and analytical observer, not as a validating instance but as integral to the
practice. (1995: 10)

Readers undertaking an action research project through an academic dissertation will engage in their own review of these philosophical issues. Suffice it to
say that action research as a scientific approach does not have to justify itself in
comparison to other approaches, but rather is evaluated within its own frame of
reference.

An integrative approach to research incorporates three voices and audiences – first, second and third person (Reason and Bradbury, 2001; Reason
and Torbert, 2001). Traditionally, research has focused on third person –
researchers doing research on third persons and writing a report for other third
persons. In a more complete vision of research as presented by action research
and many other transformational inquiry approaches, authentic third-person
research integrates first- and second-person voices. First-person research is
typically characterized as the forms of inquiry and practice that one does on
one's own and so addresses the ability of the individual to foster an inquiring
approach to his or her own life, to act out of awareness and purposefully. First-
person research can take researchers 'upstream' where they inquire into their
basic assumptions, desires, intentions and philosophy of life. It can also take
them 'downstream' where they inquire into their behaviour, ways of relating
and their action in the world. Second-person inquiry/practice addresses their
ability to inquire into and work with others on issues of mutual concern,
through face-to-face dialogue, conversation and joint action. Second person
poses an important challenge as to who is involved in the research and how. As
action research is integrally collaborative and democratic the quality of second-
person inquiry and action is central. Third-person inquiry/practice aims at
creating communities of inquiry, involving people beyond the direct second-
person action. Third person is impersonal and is actualized through dissemination
by reporting, publishing and extrapolating from the concrete to the general. As
Reason and Torbert (2001) point out there are plenty of implicit examples of
first-, second- and third-person inquiry, but what is required now is explicit
integrating of all three persons with action and inquiry. The construct of
first-, second- and third-person inquiry is a development of Reason and
Marshall's popular notion of three audiences of research:

All good research is <u>for me, for us</u>, and <u>for them</u>: it speaks to three audiences … It is <u>for them</u> to the extent that it produces some kind of

generalizable ideas and outcomes . . . It is <u>for us</u> to the extent that it responds to concerns for our praxis, is relevant and timely . . . [for] those who are struggling with problems in their field of action. It is <u>for me</u> to the extent that the process and outcomes respond directly to the individual researcher's being-in-the-world. (Reason and Marshall, 1987: 112–13)

Foundations of action research

Action research has been traditionally defined as an approach to research which is based on a collaborative problem-solving relationship between researcher and client which aims at both solving a problem and generating new knowledge. It has many origins and roots in the work of Kurt Lewin, one of the founding fathers of social psychology, in Paolo Freire's work on consciousness-raising, and in various schools of liberation thought, notably Marxist and feminist. We are building particularly on how action research developed largely from the work of Kurt Lewin and his associates, and involves a collaborative cyclical process of diagnosing a change situation or a problem, planning, gathering data, taking action, and then fact-finding about the results of that action in order to plan and take further action (Lewin, 1946, 1948; Dickens and Watkins, 1999). The key idea is that action research uses a scientific approach to study the resolution of important social or organizational issues together with those who experience these issues directly.

Argyris (1993) summarizes four core themes of Lewin's work. First, Lewin integrated theory with practice by framing social science as the study of problems of real life, and he connected all problems to theory. Second, he designed research by framing the whole, and then differentiating the parts. Third, he produced constructs which could be used to generalize and understand the individual case, particularly through the researcher as intervenor and his notion that one could only understand something when one tried to change it. Fourth, he was concerned with placing social science at the service of democracy, thereby changing the role of those being studied from subjects to clients so that help, if effective, could improve the quality of life and lead to more valid knowledge. Marrow, Lewin's biographer, states,

Theory was always an intrinsic part of Lewin's search for understanding, but theory often evolved and became refined as the data unfolded, rather than being systematically detailed in advance. Lewin was led by both data and theory, each feeding the other, each guiding the research process. (Marrow, 1969: 128)

Argyris and colleagues (1985: 8–9) summarize Lewin's concept of action research:

1   It involves change experiments on real problems in social systems. It focuses on a particular problem and seeks to provide assistance to the client system.
2   Like social management more generally, it involves iterative cycles of identifying a problem, planning, acting and evaluating.
3   The intended change in an action research project typically involves reeducation, a term that refers to changing patterns of thinking and action that are currently well established in individuals and groups. A change intended by change agents is typically at the level of norms and values expressed in action. Effective re-education depends on participation by clients in diagnosis, fact finding and free choice to engage in new kinds of action.
4   It challenges the status quo from a participative perspective, which is congruent with the requirements of effective re-education.
5   It is intended to contribute simultaneously to basic knowledge in social science and to social action in everyday life. High standards for developing theory and empirically testing propositions organized by theory are not to be sacrificed nor is the relation to practice to be lost.

After Lewin's untimely death in 1947, action research became integral to the growth of the theory and practice of organization development (Cunningham, 1993; Greenwood and Levin, 1998; French and Bell, 1999; Burke, 2002; Weisbord, 2004), and significant for organizational research (Eden and Huxham, 1996; Gummesson, 2000), such as commercial organizations (Pasmore, 2001; Coughlan and Coghlan, 2002: Adler et al., 2004), education (Zeichner, 2001), community work (Stringer, 1999) and health and social care (Morrison and Lifford, 2001; Winter and Munn-Giddings, 2001), nursing (Waterman et al., 2001) and occupational therapy (Atwal, 2003).

Lippitt (1979) distinguishes three different meanings that have been denoted by the term action research which reflect different roles played by the researcher. First, diagnostic research is conducted concerning some ongoing aspect of an action process. In this form of research the researcher gathers the data and presents it to those who are in a position to take some action. The research originates from the researcher's interests and is useful to the organization, partly as a pay-off for allowing access. In Lippitt's view this does not constitute action research. The second meaning of the term action research is connoted by a procedure of collecting data from participants of a system and providing feedback about the findings of the data as an intervention to influence, presumably in a helpful way, the ongoing action process of the system. In this model the researcher may be acting either as a data gatherer solely or in a helping role to the members of the system. The third meaning of action research is defined as a procedure in which the participants of a social system are involved in a data collection process about themselves and they utilize the data they have generated to review the facts about themselves in order to take some form of remedial or developmental action. In this model, the researcher and the researched are working in collaboration. In Lippitt's view this is the purest form of action research.

Cooperrider and Srivastva (1987) criticize how action research has developed to be viewed as a form of problem solving. They challenge what they see as underlying assumptions about the nature of action research, which are based on utilitarian and technical views of organizations as problems to be solved. As an alternative, they propose appreciative inquiry as a form of action research which focuses on building on what is already successful, rather than what is deficient.

For Gummesson (2000: 16) action research is 'the most demanding and far-reaching method of doing case study research'. He integrates the characteristics of action research from several case studies and focuses on it from a management perspective.

1   *Action researchers take action.* Action researchers are not merely observing something happening; they are actively working at making it happen.

2   *Action research always involves two goals*: solve a problem and contribute to science. As we pointed out earlier action research is about research *in* action and does not postulate a distinction between theory and action. Hence the challenge for action researchers is to engage in both making the action happen and stand back from the action and reflect on it as it happens in order to contribute theory to the body of knowledge.

3   *Action research is interactive.* Action research requires cooperation between the researchers and the client personnel, and continuous adjustment to new information and new events. In action research, the members of the client system are co-researchers as the action researcher is working with them on their issue so that the issue may be resolved or improved for their system and a contribution be made to the body of knowledge. As action research is a series of unfolding and unpredictable events, the actors need to work together and be able to adapt to the contingencies of the unfolding story.

4   *Action research aims at developing holistic understanding* during a project and recognizing complexity. As organizations are dynamic socio-technical systems, action researchers need to have a broad view of how the system works and be able to move between formal structural and technical and

informal people subsystems. Working with organizational systems requires an ability to work with dynamic complexity, which describes how a system is complex, not because of a lot of detail (detail complexity) but because of multiple causes and effects over time (Senge, 1990).

5 *Action research is fundamentally about change.* Action research is applicable to the understanding, planning and implementation of change in groups, organizations and communities. As action research is fundamentally about change, knowledge of and skill in the dynamics of organizational change are necessary. We develop this point in Chapter 8.

6 *Action research requires an understanding of the ethical framework*, values and norms within which it is used in a particular context. In action research ethics involves authentic relationships between the action researcher and the members of the client system as to how they understand the process and take significant action. Values and norms that flow from such ethical principles typically focus on how the action researcher works with the members of the organization. We will develop this point in Chapter 6.

7 *Action research can include all types of data gathering methods.* Action research does not preclude the use of data gathering methods from traditional research. Qualitative and quantitative tools, such as interviews and surveys are commonly used. What is important in action research is that the planning and use of these tools be well thought out with the members of the organization and be clearly integrated into the action research process. We return to this point in Chapter 8.

8 *Action research requires a breadth of preunderstanding* of the corporate or organizational environment, the conditions of business or service delivery, the structure and dynamics of operating systems and the theoretical underpinnings of such systems. Preunderstanding refers to the knowledge the action researcher brings to the research project. Such a need for preunderstanding signals that an action research approach is inappropriate for researchers who, for example, think that all they have to do to develop grounded theory is just to go out into the field.

9 *Action research should be conducted in real time*, though retrospective action research is also acceptable. While action research is a live case study being written as it unfolds, it can also take the form of a traditional case study written in retrospect, when the written case is used as an intervention into the organization in the present. In such a situation the case performs the function of a 'learning history' and is used as an intervention to promote reflection and learning in the organization (Kleiner and Roth, 1997).

10 *The action research paradigm requires its own quality criteria.* Action research should *not* be judged by the criteria of positivist science, but rather within the criteria of its own terms.

Business consultancy language not withstanding, Gummesson's characteristics apply to the action researcher in any organization. The research project unfolds as the cycles of planning, data gathering, taking action, reviewing and further planning and action are enacted.

Shani and Pasmore (1985) present a complete theory of the action research process in terms of four factors:

1 *Context*: These factors set the context of the action research project. Individual goals may differ and impact the direction of the project, while shared goals enhance collaboration. Organizational characteristics, such as resources, history, formal and informal organizations and the degrees of congruence between them affect the readiness and capability for participating in action research. Environmental factors in the global and local economies provide the larger context in which action research takes place.
2 *Quality of relationships*: The quality of relationship between members and researchers is paramount. Hence the relationships need to be managed through trust, concern for other, equality of influence, common language.
3 *Quality of the action research process itself*: The quality of the action research process is grounded in the dual focus on both the inquiry process and the implementation process.
4 *Outcomes*: The dual outcomes of action research are some level of improvement and the development of self-help and competencies out of the action and the creation of new knowledge from the inquiry.

Experiential paradigms of action research

The term action research is a generic one and is used to refer to a bewildering array of activities and methods. At its core, action research is a research approach which focuses on simultaneous action and research in a collaborative manner. Within this approach are multiple paradigms or methodologies, each of which has its own distinctive emphasis (Greenwood and Levin, 1998; Adler et al., 2004). Some action research methodologies have developed from sociology and focus on how communities as socio–political systems enact social change. These approaches have a focus outside of the organizational context and tend to address structural emancipatory issues, relating to, for example, education, social exclusion and power and control (Lynch, 1999; Fals-Borda, 2001). This tradition of action research is particularly associated with action research in the southern hemisphere. Other action research approaches, particularly in the northern hemisphere, have their origins in applied behavioural science and have developed in the organizational context (Coch and French, 1948; Foster, 1972; Schein, 1987; French and Bell, 1999; Coghlan and Coughlan, 2003; Adler et al., 2004). Parallel to this approach is one that focuses on relationships, both in the workplace and between social partners in regional development (Gustavsen, 1992, 2001; Eikeland and Finstrud, 1995; Toulmin and Gustavsen, 1996). The central process for building relationships is democratic dialogue. This book is addressed primarily to those working within organizational settings and as such is part of the northern hemisphere tradition of action research.

A significant feature of all action research is that the purpose of research is not simply or even primarily to contribute to the fund of knowledge in a field, or even to develop emancipatory theory, but rather to forge a more direct link between intellectual knowledge/theory and action so that each inquiry contributes directly to the flourishing of human persons, and their communities (Reason and Torbert, 2001). Action research rejects the separation between thought and action that underlies the pure–applied distinction that has traditionally characterized management and social research. These approaches incorporate a collaborative enactment of action research cycles whereby the intended research outcome is the construction of actionable knowledge.

In this chapter we will not elaborate on the nuances between the different action research approaches as they are well articulated elsewhere (Whyte, 1991; Elden and Chisholm, 1993; Brooks and Watkins, 1994; Raelin, 1997, 1999; Greenwood and Levin, 1998; Bray et al., 2000; Adler et al., 2004). We are not focusing on differences or even instances of these differences, but rather the core values and processes that are central across each of these approaches.

Traditional action research

Action research in its traditional sense comes from the work of Kurt Lewin (1946, 1948) and involves a collaborative change management or problem-solving relationship between researcher and client aimed at both solving a problem and generating new knowledge. The researcher and client engage in collaborative cycles of planning, taking action and evaluating. This form of action research is central to the theory and practice of organization development (Cunningham, 1993; French and Bell, 1999; Coghlan and McAuliffe, 2003). It is this form of action research that provides the central theme of this book.

Participatory action research

Participatory action research (PAR) typically has a focus outside of the organizational context and involves egalitarian participation by a community to transform some aspects of its situation or structures. It focuses on concerns of power and powerlessness and how the powerless are excluded from decision making, and moves to empowering people to construct and use their own knowledge (Selener, 1997; Fals-Borda, 2001). Many of the liberation or emancipatory action research approaches are variations on PAR.

Action learning

Action learning is an approach to the development of people in organizations which takes the task as the vehicle for learning. It reverses the traditional learning process where one learns something first and then applies it. In action learning the starting point is the action. It is based on two principles. First, 'There can be no learning without action and no (sober and deliberate) action without learning' (Revans, 1998: 83). Second, 'Those unable to change themselves cannot change what goes on around them' (Revans, 1998: 85). Its three objectives are outlined by Revans, the founder of action learning:

1   To make useful progress on the treatment of some real problems or opportunity.
2   To give nominated managers sufficient scope to learn for themselves in the company of others.
3   To encourage teachers and others in management development to help others learn with and from each other.

Action learning is formulated around Revans's learning formula, $L = P + Q$ (Revans, 1998). L stands for learning, P for programmed learning (i.e. current knowledge in use, already known, what is in books etc.) and Q for questioning insight. Revans (1982) describes three processes central to action learning:

1   A process of inquiry into the issue under consideration – its history, manifestation, what has prevented it from being resolved, what has previously been attempted. Revans calls this process System Alpha.
2   Action learning is science in progress through rigorous exploration of the resolution of the issue through action and reflection. He calls this System Beta.

3   Action learning is characterized by a quality of group interaction which enables individual critical reflection, and ultimately the learning. This is the essence of action learning and Revans calls it System Gamma.

These three processes emphasize how action learning involves engagement with real issues, rather than with fabrications, is both scientifically rigorous in confronting the issue and critically subjective through managers learning in action. Participating managers take responsibility for and control of their own learning and so there is minimal use of experts (Pedler, 1996; Revans, 1998; Dilworth and Willis, 2003).

Action science

Action science is associated with the work of Chris Argyris (Argyris et al., 1985; Friedman, 2001a; Argyris, 2004). Argyris places an emphasis on the cognitive processes of individuals' 'theories-in-use', which he describes in terms of Model I (strategies of control, self-protection, defensiveness and covering up embarrassment) and Model II (strategies eliciting valid information, free choice and commitment). Attention to how individuals' theories-in-use create organizational defensiveness is an important approach to organizational learning (Argyris, 1990, 1999; Argyris and Schon, 1996; Senge, 1990; Senge et al., 1994).

Developmental action inquiry

Developmental action inquiry is associated with the work of Bill Torbert (1987, 1991, 1999, 2001; Fisher et al., 2000). Torbert defines action inquiry as 'a kind of scientific inquiry that is conducted in everyday life . . . that deals primarily with "primary" data encountered "on-line" in the midst of perception and action' (1991: 220). Torbert develops the inquiry process by linking the ability to engage in the rigour of action inquiry with stages of ego development. As individuals advance through stages of ego development they may develop the skills that confront them at those stages. As Torbert (1999) illustrates, the goal orientation of the Achiever stage can evolve into the self-conscious responsiveness of the Strategist stage. In his view, it is in the latter stages of development that individuals can engage in collaborative inquiry, whereby as individuals they reflect on their behaviour-in-action, and their behaviour towards others is such that it invites them to do likewise. Such behaviour has implications for the role of leadership and the use of power in creating communities of inquiry (Torbert, 1987, 1989).

Cooperative inquiry

One of the forms that action research takes is cooperative inquiry (Reason, 1988, 1999; Heron, 1996; Heron and Reason, 2001). Heron and Reason define cooperative inquiry:

> as involving two or more people researching a topic through their own experience of it in order to:
>
> - understand their world to make sense of their life and develop new and creative ways of looking at things.
> - learn how to act to change things they might want to change and find out how to do things better. (Heron and Reason, 2001: 179)

Each person 'is a co-subject in the experience phases and co-researcher in the reflection phases' (Heron, 1996; 1). Reason (1999) set out the process of co-operative inquiry in the following stages.

1   The group talks about the group's interests and concerns, agrees on the focus of the inquiry, and develops together a set of questions or proposals its members wish to explore.
2   The group applies actions in the everyday work of the members, who initiate the actions and observe and record the outcomes of their own and each other's behaviour.
3   The group members as co-researchers become fully immersed in their experience. They may deepen into the experience or they may be led away from the original ideas and proposals into new fields, unpredicted action and creative insights.
4   After an agreed period engaged in phases two and three, the co-researchers reassemble to consider their original questions in the light of their experience.

Clinical inquiry

In writing about an organization development approach to organizational research, Schein (1987, 2001) introduces the notion of the 'clinical' approach to research. For Schein, clinical refers to those trained helpers (such as clinical and counselling psychologists, social workers, organization development consultants) who work professionally with human systems. These trained helpers act as organizational clinicians in that they: (a) emphasize in-depth observation of learning and change processes; (b) emphasize the effects of interventions; (c) operate from models of what it is to function as a healthy system and focus on pathologies, puzzles and anomalies which illustrate deviations from healthy functioning; (d) build theory and empirical knowledge through developing concepts which capture the real dynamics of systems (Schein, 1997).

Appreciative inquiry

Appreciative inquiry has emerged from the work of Cooperrider, and aims at large system change through an appreciative focus on what already works in a system, rather than a focus on what is deficient (Cooperrider et al., 2000, 2003; Golembiewski, 1998; Ludema et al., 2001, 2003). It is built around four phases:

1   *Discovery*: appreciating the best of 'what is'.
2   *Dream*: envisioning 'what could be'.
3   *Design*: co-constructing 'what should be'.
4   *Destiny*: sustaining 'what will be'.

Appreciative inquiry takes a counter view to clinical inquiry through its focus on appreciation rather than pathologies and problems.

Learning history

A learning history is a document composed by participants in a change effort, with the help of external consultants who act as 'learning historians' (Kleiner and Roth, 1997, 2000; Roth and Kleiner, 1998, 2000). It presents the experiences and understandings in the words of those who have gone through and/or been affected by the change in order to help the organization move forward. The learning history is an action research process by being an intervention into the organization. This happens when the action research documentation is made available to organizational stakeholders as 'a written narrative of a company's recent set of critical episodes' (Kleiner and Roth, 1997: 173) with the purpose of facilitating learning. Kleiner and Roth (1997) present a framework for how this might be done. The narrative is read by significant stakeholders who contribute to the story from their perspective in a special right-hand column on the page. Those social scientists and 'learning historians' who study the narrative use a left-hand column for their reflection and analysis as the basis for further discussion in the organization.

Reflective practice

Reflective practice refers to how individuals engage in critical reflection on their own action. It is associated with the work of Schon (1983, 1987, 1991; Jarvis, 1999; Raelin, 2000). Reflective practice may be a specific dimension of action research, as indeed we will argue in the next chapter, but by and large published accounts of reflective practice focus only on the individual and generally do not consider any organizational dynamics or outcomes related to the individual's action.

Schon (1983) reflects on four ways that reflective practitioners might engage in 'reflective research'

1   *Frame analysis*: when practitioners become aware of their 'frames' and consider alternatives.
2   *Repertoire building research*: accumulating and describing examples of reflection in action.
3   *Research on fundamental methods of inquiry and overarching theories*: by examining episodes of practice in an action science.
4   *Research on the process of reflection in action*: studying processes whereby practitioners learn to reflect in action.

Evaluative inquiry

Closely related to action research is the process of evaluative inquiry which is a reformulation of traditional evaluation practices through an emphasis on using the process of inquiry to generate organizational learning (Preskill and Torres, 1999). Many of the processes within action research, such as collaborative inquiry, reflection, joint planning and taking action are utilized as interventions to shape how projects are evaluated in order to stimulate organizational learning.

For the neophyte reader these multiple methodologies are confusing. In our view, it is important to emphasize that these different methodologies are not mutually exclusive. They are sets of general principles and devices which can be adapted to different research issues and contexts. Each has its own emphasis and can be appropriately used in conjunction with other approaches. What is important is that you, as the action researcher, be helped to seek the method appropriate to your inquiry and situation.

Conclusions

In this chapter we have outlined the foundations of action research as research that is based on a collaborative problem-solving relationship between researcher and client which aims at both solving a problem and generating new knowledge. Irrespective of methodological or epistemological perspective, how to distinguish good research from bad is the key question. Generally speaking, good research is purposeful, its goals are clearly defined and significant, the methodological procedures defensible, evidence is systematically analysed and the 'objectivity' of the researcher clearly evident.

Action research is an approach to research that works at gathering data in the field by non-traditional methods with the concerns of practitioners who want to improve organizations and communities. Regretfully, it has often become a glib term for involving clients in research and has lost its role as a powerful conceptual tool for uncovering truth on which action can be taken. Action research is a form of science, which differs from the model of experimental physics, but is genuinely scientific in its emphasis on careful observation and study of the effects of behaviour on human systems as their members manage change. Action research and the action research cycle is discussed in detail in Chapter 2.

2

Enacting the Action Research Cycle

In its original Lewinian and simplest form, the action research cycle comprises a pre-step and three core activities: planning, action and fact finding (Lewin, 1946). The pre-step involves naming the general objective. Planning comprises having an overall plan and a decision regarding what the first step to take is. Action involves taking that first step, and fact finding involves evaluating the first step, seeing what was learned and creating the basis for correcting the next step. So there is a continuing 'spiral of steps, each of which is composed of a circle of planning, action and fact-finding about the result of the action' (Lewin, 1946: 146).

These core steps have been articulated differently by different authors, from Stringer's (1999) simple *look, think, act,* to French and Bell's (1999) complex action research organization development framework involving iterative cycles of joint action planning, feedback, further data gathering, diagnosis and action of an external OD consultant with a client system.

The action research cycle

For the context of doing action research in your own organization we are presenting an action research cycle comprising a pre-step, context/purpose and four basic steps, diagnosing, planning action, taking action, and evaluating action (see Figure 2.1). The exploration of the action research cycle needs to be understood in terms of the four factors of action research presented in Chapter 1: context, quality of relationships, quality of the action research process itself and the outcomes.

Pre-step: context and purpose

The action research cycle unfolds in real time and begins with an understanding of the context of the project. Why is this project necessary or desirable? In

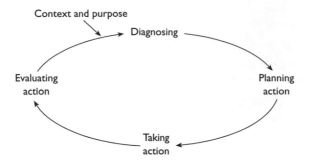

FIGURE 2.1 **THE ACTION RESEARCH CYCLE**

terms of assessing the external context, what are the economic, political and social forces driving change? In terms of internal forces, what are the cultural and structural forces driving change? The assessment of these forces identifies their source, their potency and the nature of the demands they make on the system. Included also is the assessment of the degree of choice in how the system responds to the forces for change. Once a sense of the need or desirability for the project is identified, then the most useful focus for attention is the definition of a desired future state. The process of defining the desired future state is critical as it sets the boundaries for the purpose of the project and helps provide focus and energy for the later stages. The issues are elaborated in Chapter 8.

Another critical consideration in this pre-step is the establishment of collaborative relationships with those who have ownership or need to have ownership of the above questions. A central second-person task in this regard is to develop the groups or groups with which you will be working on the project.

Main Steps

Diagnosing

Diagnosing involves naming what the issues are, however provisionally, as a working theme, on the basis of which action will be planned and taken. As diagnosis involves the articulation of the theoretical foundations of action, it needs to be done carefully and thoroughly. While the diagnosis may change in later iterations of the action research cycle, any changes in diagnosis need to be recorded and articulated clearly, showing how events have led to alternative diagnosis and showing the evidence and rationale for the new diagnosis on which further action is based. It is important that the diagnosing step be a collaborative venture, that is, that you as the action researcher engage relevant others in the process of diagnosis and not be the expert who does the diagnosis apart from others. In Chapter 7 we focus on how a project may be framed and in Chapter 10 we outline some guidelines for using diagnostic frameworks.

Planning action

Planning action follows from the analysis of the context and purpose of the project, the framing of the issue and the diagnosis, and is consistent with them. It may be that this action planning focuses on a first step or a series of first steps. In Chapter 8 we will describe how you implement the action research project. Again we emphasize the importance of collaboration in planning action.

Taking action

Then the plans are implemented and interventions are made.

Evaluating action

The outcomes of the action, both intended and unintended, are examined with a view to seeing:

- if the original diagnosis was correct;
- if the action taken was correct;
- if the action was taken in an appropriate manner;
- what feeds into the next cycle of diagnosis, planning and action.

So the cycle continues (see Figure 2.2).

In any action research project there are multiple action research cycles operating concurrently. These cycles typically have different time spans. The image of a clock captures this usefully (see Figure 2.3). The hour hand, which takes twelve hours to complete its cycle, may represent the project as a whole which may take several years to complete its cycle. The minute hand, which takes an hour to complete its cycle, may represent phases or particular sections of the project. The second hand, which completes its cycle in a minute, may represent

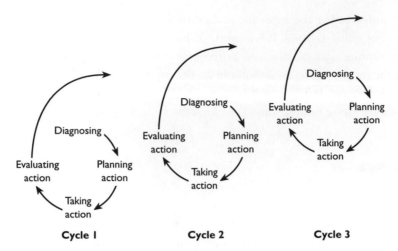

FIGURE 2.2 **SPIRAL OF ACTION RESEARCH CYCLES**

specific actions within the project, such as a specific meeting or interview. As in the clock, where the revolutions of the three hands are concurrent and where the revolutions of the second hand enable the revolutions of the minute hand and the revolutions of the second and minute hands enable the completion of the hour hand, the short-term action research cycles contribute to the medium-term cycles which contribute to the longer-term cycle.

FIGURE 2.3 **CONCURRENT CYCLES OF ACTION RESEARCH**

While the action research cycle expresses the core process of integrating action and theory it is important to keep it in perspective. For instance, Heron (1996) describes two approaches to the use of the cycle. He contrasts one approach, *Apollonian* whereby the cycles are enacted in a rational, linear, systematic manner with *Dionysian*, an approach where there is an imaginative, expressive, tacit approach to integrating reflection and action. He cautions against being rigid in adapting the action research cycle formally and so denying spontaneity and creativity. It is also important not to get too preoccupied in the cycles at the expense of the quality of participation.

Meta learning

In any action research project there are two action research cycles operating in parallel. One is the cycle we have just described of diagnosing, planning, taking action and evaluating in relation to the project. Zuber-Skerritt and Perry (2002) call this the 'core' action research cycle. The second is a reflection cycle which is an action research cycle about the action research cycle. Zuber-Skerritt and Perry call this the 'thesis' action research cycle. In other words, at the same time as you are engaging in the project or core action research cycles, you need to be diagnosing, planning, taking action and evaluating about how the action research project itself is going and what you are learning. You need to be continually inquiring into each of the four main steps, asking how these steps are being conducted and how they are consistent with each other and, so, shaping how the subsequent steps are conducted. As Chris Argyris (2003) argues in making the same point, this inquiry into the steps of the cycles themselves is central to the development of actionable knowledge. It is the dynamic of this reflection on reflection that incorporates the learning process of the action research cycle and enables action research to be more than everyday problem solving. Hence it is learning about learning, in other word, meta learning.

Mezirow (1991) identifies three forms of reflection: content, process and premise. These are useful categories. *Content* reflection is where you think about the issues, what is happening and so on. *Process* reflection is where you think about strategies, procedures and how things are being done. *Premise* reflection is where you critique underlying assumptions and perspectives. All three forms of reflection are critical.

When content, process and premise reflections are applied to the action research cycle, they form the meta cycle of inquiry (see Figure 2.4). The *content* of what is diagnosed, planned, acted on and evaluated is studied and evaluated. The *process* of how diagnosis is undertaken, how action planning

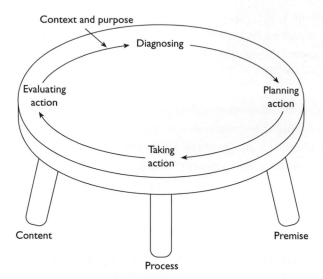

FIGURE 2.4 **META CYCLE OF INQUIRY**

flows from that diagnosis and is conducted, how actions follow and are an implementation of the stated plans and how evaluation is conducted are critical foci for inquiry. There is also *premise* reflection, which is inquiry into the unstated, and often non-conscious, underlying assumptions which govern attitudes and behaviour. For instance, the culture of the organization or subculture of the group working on the project has a powerful impact on how issues are viewed and discussed, without members being aware of them (Schein, 1992, 1996a, 1999b).

If you are writing a dissertation, the meta cycle is the focus of your dissertation. Remember, the action research project and your dissertation are not identical. They are integrally interlinked, but they are not the same. The project on which you are working may go ahead irrespective of whether or not you are writing a dissertation. Your dissertation is an inquiry into the project, hence you need to describe both cycles in a way that demonstrates the quality of rigour of your inquiry.

Mezirow's forms of reflection parallel the four territories of experience commonly used in action research (Fisher et al., 2000; Reason and Torbert, 2001; Torbert, 2001). These four territories operate at the individual, interpersonal and organizational levels:

1 *Intentions*: purpose, goals, aims and vision.
2 *Planning*: plans, strategy, tactics, schemes.

3   *Action*: implementation, performance.
4   *Outcomes*: results, outcomes, consequences and effects.

Action research aims to develop awareness, understanding and skills across all these territories. You try to understand your intentions, to develop appropriate plans and strategies, to be skilled at carrying them out, to reflect on how well you have carried out the plans, and to evaluate their results. You can also inquire about the connections between these phases. You might, for example, begin with the outcomes, and explore how your actions caused these outcomes. Or you may take the inquiry further, and look at how your intentions and plans shaped your actions.

The activities of the meta cycle are not confined to your first-person practice as the individual action researcher. To add another layer of complexity to the learning cycle, the second-person practice with the groups and teams engaged in the action research cycles also attends to the steps of content, process and premise reflection.

Attending to the action research cycle and to the meta cycle may involve more than simply attending to behaviour. You may draw from techniques in the qualitative research approaches through how you formulate the issue, collect and analyse data and report results (Sagor 1992). Techniques from grounded theory approaches may be useful once the core compatibilities and incompatibilities between the two approaches are recognized (Baskerville and Pries-Heje, 1999).

Quality and rigour in action research

The action research paradigm requires its own quality criteria. Action research should *not* be judged by the criteria of positivist science, but rather within the criteria of its own terms. Reason and Bradbury (2001) point to what they consider to be choice points and questions for quality in action research:

1   Is the action research explicit in developing a praxis of relational participation? In other words how well does the action research reflect the cooperation between the action researcher and the members of the organization?
2   Is action research guided by a reflexive concern for practical outcomes? Is the action project governed by constant and iterative reflection as part of the process of organizational change or improvement?
3   Does action research include a plurality of knowing which ensures

conceptual-theoretical integrity, extends our ways of knowing and has a methodological appropriateness? Action research is inclusive of practical, propositional, presentational and experiential knowing and so as a methodology is appropriate to furthering knowledge on different levels.

4   Does action research engage in significant work? The significance of the project is an important quality in action research.

5   Does the action research result in new and enduring infrastructures? In other words, does sustainable change come out of the project?

Reason (2003) argues that as an action researcher you need to be aware of these choices and make them clear and transparent to yourself and to those with whom you are engaging in inquiry and to those to whom you present your research in writing or presentations. The editorial guidelines for the journal *Action Research* invite potential contributors to address these dimensions explicitly in submitting their work to the journal.

Rigour in action research refers to how data are generated, gathered, explored and evaluated, how events are questioned and interpreted through multiple action research cycles. In other words, as the action researcher, you need to show:

1   How you engaged in the steps of multiple and repetitious action research cycles (how diagnosing, planning, taking action and evaluating were done), and how these were recorded to reflect that they are a true representation of what was studied.

2   How you challenged and tested your own assumptions and interpretations of what was happening continuously through the project, by means of content, process and premise reflection, so that your familiarity with and closeness to the issues are exposed to critique.

3   How you accessed different views of what was happening which probably produced both confirming and contradictory interpretations.

4   How your interpretations and diagnoses are grounded in scholarly theory, rigorously applied, and how project outcomes are challenged, supported or disconfirmed in terms of the theories underpinning those interpretations and diagnoses.

The value in action research is not whether the change process was successful or not, but rather that the exploration of the data – that is how a particular change was managed – provides useful and interesting theory which may contribute to learning on the subject of change management.

What does a good action research project look like? Eden and Huxham

(1996) provide an extensive list of the fifteen characteristics of good action research. The foundational characteristics reflect the intentionality of the researcher to change an organization, that the project has some implications beyond those involved directly in it and that the project has an explicit aim to elaborate or develop theory as well as be useful to the organization. Theory must inform the design and development of the actions. Eden and Huxham place great emphasis on the enactment of the action research cycles, in which systematic method and orderliness is required in reflecting on the outcomes of each cycle and the design of the subsequent cycles.

In our view a good action research project contains three main elements: a good story; rigorous reflection on that story; and an extrapolation of usable knowledge or theory from the reflection on the story. These can be put in terms of three questions: What happened? How you do make sense of what happened? So what?

What happened?

As action research is about real time change, its core is the story of what takes place. The action research cycle of the general objective pre-step, and the three main steps of planning, action and fact finding describe how the project is conceived, what is intended, the cycles of action and the outcomes, both intended and unintended. The story must be presented in a factual and neutral manner, that is to say, as if it had been recorded on camera, and so that all the actors could agree on what had taken place. In short, the story is based on directly observable behaviour. Therefore, you need to be able to present evidence to support your narrative. Recorded data in journals and organizational documentation are important supporting evidence.

Accordingly, it is critical that fact be clearly distinguished from value, that the basic story does not contain the author's inferences or interpretations, or at least, not without such inferences or interpretations being explicitly identified as such. For instance, if an action research story contains an assertion that a certain group was out to wreck the project, the narrative would need to be clear that there was evidence that group was trying to wreck the project, rather than it being an inference of the researcher or any party who saw itself as victim of that group's action. We explore the role of making inferences in Chapter 3.

How you do make sense of what happened?

The critical process with respect to articulating your sense-making is making your tacit knowledge explicit. This involves not only providing an analysis of what you think is going on in the story, but also of how you are making sense of it as the story unfolds (Weick, 1995). In other words, sense-making is not only a retrospective process, but is also a process which is concurrent with the story, and in terms of the action research cycle actually shapes the story. Hence the image we used in Chapter 1 of the action researcher as actor–director. As you report assumptions which you held as the story progressed, you need to show how you tested them, especially if these assumptions were privately held. In terms of our example above, the researcher needs to test whether or not the group, which he thinks is out to wreck the project, actually intends that.

So what?

The third issue in action research is how the action research project is contributing theory or usable knowledge. As action research is context bound in a particular setting and set of events it needs to have some interest and relevance to the uninvolved reader, the third-person readership. Hence, the question 'so what?' is a pertinent and challenging question or as Friedman (2001a: 168) put it, 'if . . . then . . .'.

Conclusions

In summary, enacting the action research cycle involves not only the pre-step of articulating the context and purpose of the project, and the main steps of diagnosing, planning action, taking action and evaluating, but also reflecting on content, process and premise issues in how the action research cycles are undertaken. Both the action research and meta learning are undertaken by individuals, teams, between teams in the interdepartmental groups and between organizations. The rigour of your inquiry is demonstrated by how you expose these activities to critique and how your conclusions are supported by your development of theory or usable knowledge. We will now turn to how you as the action researcher can engage in learning in action.

1 Select an issue/problem that you have worked on in your team (or are working on).

2 What is the *context* of this issue? Why is it important? What are the stakes involved?

3 Describe how the issue was *diagnosed*. How did you decide that an intervention was needed or wanted/what was wrong, what the causes were? How did you deal with different diagnoses in the team?

4 What action was *planned*?

5 What happened when the action was *implemented*? What were the outcomes, both intended and unintended?

6 How did the team *review* the outcomes?

7 What was then diagnosed, planned, implemented etc.?

8 What is the *meta learning* from this exercise?

(a) As you look back on this, what strikes you about the *content* of the issue? Was the diagnosis correct? Had you named the right issue? What have you learned about this issue in your business/organization?

(b) What strikes you about *process*? How did the team work on the issue? What have you learned about how to plan, take action and evaluate?

(c) Was there any challenge to existing *premises* of how you thought about things, anything in the event that challenged the team to ask different questions, see the issue in terms of a different category of issue/problem, and so on?

Exercise 2.1
Enacting the action research cycles (from Figure 2.1)

3 Learning in Action

In this chapter we explore how you, as the insider action researcher, engage in the action research cycles of diagnosing, planning action, taking action and evaluating action. How do you learn in action? How do you attend to what you might be learning as you engage in the issues of your action research project? As answers to these questions, we outline some processes of how adults learn in action and how reflection and journalling may be used to help you realize what and how you are learning. Our focus is not on learning *on* action but on learning *in* action.

Action research distinguishes four kinds of knowing, reflecting different ways in which we deal with and act within the world (Heron, 1996; Reason and Torbert, 2001):

1 *Experiential knowing*: the knowledge arising as we encounter the realities around us.
2 *Presentational knowing*: the knowledge expressed in our giving form to this experiential knowing, through language, images, music, painting and the like.
3 *Propositional knowing*: the knowledge distilling our experiential and presentational knowing into theories, statements and propositions distilling.
4 *Practical knowing*: the knowledge that brings the other three forms of knowing to full fruition by *doing* appropriate things, skilfully and competently.

The form of knowledge that action research aims to produce is practical knowing, the knowing that shapes the quality of your moment-to-moment action. A key process, therefore, is how you come to this knowledge or how you learn in action.

Learning in action is grounded in the inquiry–reflection process. Schon's (1983, 1987) notion of the 'reflective practitioner' captures the essentials of knowing-in-action and reflection-in-action. Knowing-in-action is tacit and opens up outcomes that fall into the boundaries of what you have learned to treat as normal. Reflection-in-action occurs when you are in the middle of an action and you ask questions about what you are doing. The outcome is immediate as it leads to an on the spot adjustment of your action.

Inquiry can be focused outward (e.g. what is going on in the organization, in the team etc.?) or inward (e.g. what is going on in me?). In Chapter 10 we outline some conceptual frameworks which provide a basis for organizational diagnosis which are utilized for that outward focused inquiry and reflection. Here we focus on the introspective activities of inward inquiry and reflection. Judi Marshall (1999, 2001) presents individual learning in action as 'inquiry as a way of being' and describes this first-person research/practice in terms of: inquiring into the inner and outer arcs of attention; engaging in cycles of action and reflection; and being active and receptive.

Experiential learning

As the insider action researcher, you are an actor in the setting of the organization. In contrast with traditional research approaches, you are not neutral but an active intervenor making and helping things happen. Accordingly, a critical feature of action research is how you learn about yourself in action as you engage in first-, second- and third-person inquiry.

How do adults learn? We are presenting four activities: experiencing, reflecting, interpreting and taking action (Coghlan, 1997) (see Figure 3.1).

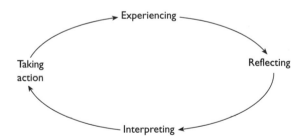

FIGURE 3.1 **THE EXPERIENTIAL LEARNING CYCLE**

Experiencing

As the action researcher you experience a great deal as the project goes through its cycles. Some of your experiences are planned, others unplanned. Some are what is done to you by others. Some experiences are cognitive; they occur through the intellectual processes of thinking and understanding. Some occur in feelings and emotions. At times you may feel excited, angry, frustrated, sad, lonely and so on. Other experiences may be experienced in the body – excited energy, embarrassed blushing, tightness in the stomach, headaches, ulcers or sickness. These three domains – cognitive, feelings and body awareness – are where experiencing occurs and you can learn by attending to these. Chandler and Torbert (2003) reflect on how first-, second- and third-person inquiry and action constitute both voice and practice and relate them to past, present and future. So for example, you may engage in first-person reflection on past events, attend to present experiences and personal intentions for the future. In your project you are experiencing what it is like to engage in diagnosing, planning action, taking action and evaluating action.

Reflecting

Attending to experience is the first step to learning. The second step is to stand back from these experiences and inquire into them. What is it that has me feeling angry? What is it that I do not yet understand? You are reflecting on your experiences of diagnosing, planning action, taking action and evaluating action in the project.

Interpreting

Interpreting is where you find answers to the questions posed in the reflection. You draw on theories and constructs to help you make sense of your experience. How do you understand what is happening in the processes of diagnosing, planning action, taking action and evaluating action?

Taking action

What do you do as a result of your reflecting and interpreting? It may be that you decide to behave differently the next time you are in a similar situation in order not to repeat the previous experience or in order to create a different outcome. What actions are you taking as a consequence of your reflection on diagnosing, planning action, taking action and evaluating action?

These four activities operate as a cycle where experiencing, reflecting, interpreting and taking action set up another cycle of experiencing, and so on. Learning becomes a continuous cycle through life. Learning is not any one of these four activities on its own but each of them together. You need to develop skills at each activity: be able to experience directly, be able to stand back and ask questions, be able to conceptualize answers to your questions, and be able to take risks and experiment in similar or new situations.

You may block learning at each activity. You may view experiencing as something predictable, routine and uninvolving from which you are detached. You may see reflecting as a luxury, an activity for which you do not have any time. You may disregard the conceptualization which accompanies interpreting as something for academics and apart from the 'real world'. You may not engage in taking new action because of a fear of taking risks or of rocking the boat. These are ways in which you may close yourself to learning.

Because the action research project and your own research project are not identical, you are engaging in an experiential learning cycle on the action research cycle (see Figure 3.2). So you are experiencing what it is like to engage in diagnosing, planning, action, taking action and evaluating, and continuously reflecting and interpreting and taking action within those activities.

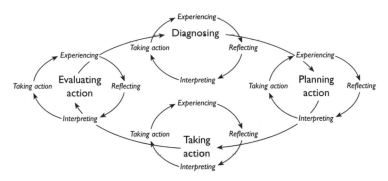

FIGURE 3.2 **THE EXPERIENTIAL LEARNING CYCLE IN ACTION RESEARCH PROJECTS**

Reflection

Reflection is the process of stepping back from experience to process what the experience means, with a view to planning further action (Kolb, 1984; Seibert and Daudelin, 1999; Raelin, 2000; Rudolph et al., 2001; McGill and Brockbank, 2004). It is the critical link between the concrete experience, the interpretation and taking new action. As Raelin (2000) discusses, it is the key to learning as it enables you to develop an ability to uncover and make explicit to yourself what you have planned, discovered and achieved in practice. He also argues that reflection must be brought into the open so that it goes beyond your privately held taken-for-granted assumptions and helps you to see how your knowledge is constructed. In action research, reflection is the activity which integrates action and research. As we discussed in Chapter 2, reflection on content, process and premise is critical to both the action research cycle and to the meta learning.

A good deal of our reflection is reflection *on* action, that is, it is a retrospective look at what has happened. Darling and Parry (2000) illustrate in their application of 'after action review' (AAR) to the US American military how post-mortems can move from being a review of the past to a living practice that anticipates issues and generates emergent learning *in* action.

Action science and developmental action inquiry, introduced in Chapter 1, provide focused approaches to attending to individual learning in action. In action science, you focus on how your actions tend to produce defensiveness and undesired outcomes, the opposite of what you intend. This happens because we hold assumptions which govern our behaviour, and we make private inferences and attributions about the motives and thought processes of others which we do not test. Accordingly, the core of the action science is learning how to identify the assumptions which govern behaviour and develop skills at testing assumptions and inferences, while at the same time exposing our own privately held theories to public testing.

The ladder of inference plots how meanings and assumptions are attributed to selected observable data and experiences, and conclusions and beliefs are adopted on which actions are based (Argyris et al., 1985; Ross, 1994). For example, at a team meeting you make a proposal for action. One of your colleagues, Joe, doesn't say anything. You think he looks as if he is sulking and conclude that he is sulking because his proposal has not been considered. Accordingly, you decide that Joe won't be on your side and that you cannot rely on him for support and subsequently you do not inform him of meetings as the project progresses. What has happened here is that you observed an event, namely, colleagues responding to your proposal. You selected part of that event (Joe not speaking) and added your own interpretations and meaning, which you did share or test, and then your own subsequent actions of excluding Joe from further meetings were based on the beliefs and assumptions deduced from your private interpretation. In terms of the image of a ladder, you have ascended the steps of inference, from the bottom rung of what is directly observable behaviour to upper rungs of acting on privately held, untested inferences.

Argyris's (1993, 2004; Argyris et al., 1985) technique of right-hand/left-hand column provides a useful technique for you to uncover your own privately held inferences and attributions in second-person practice. He suggests that you take a page on which you write down the progress of a conversation you have with another person, with whom you are working on your project. Then on another page or column you write down what you have been thinking privately about what is being said in the conversation and you have *not* said. By this method you can learn to identify how you make inferences and attributions privately in your own head out of what is rather hazy evidence and how you act on them by what you say in response.

Another useful construct to support learning in action is the notion of cognitive distortions, whereby you may become aware of how you might be prone to distorting reality, particularly when under pressure (Coghlan and Rashford, 1990). You may distort reality when you engage in such activities as: over-generalization, all-or-nothing thinking, mental filtering, jumping to conclusions, emotional reasoning, fortune telling and other similar ways of misperceiving what is happening. Distortions such as these impair your ability to engage in inquiry in action.

Emotions as well as thoughts are part of the reflective process. You need to be able to recognize and acknowledge the role feelings play in the formation of judgement and in taking action. *Focusing* (Gendlin, 1981; Cornell, 1996) provides a valuable method of listening to experiences within the body by noticing how you feel and by having a conversation with that feeling in a friendly way. It is a process of listening to your body in a gentle accepting way and hearing the messages that your inner self is sending through your body.

Developing reflective skills through journalling

Journal keeping is a significant mechanism for developing reflective skills. You note your observations and experiences in a journal and over time learn to differentiate between different experiences and ways of dealing with them. Journal keeping helps you to reflect on experiences, see how you think about them and anticipate future experiences before you undertake them (Moon, 1999; Raelin, 2000). It enables you to integrate information and experiences which, when understood, help you understand your reasoning processes and consequent behaviour and so anticipate experiences before embarking on them. Keeping a journal regularly imposes a discipline and captures your experience of key events close to when they happen and before the passage of time changes your perception of them. McNiff and colleagues (1996) describe some of the useful functions a journal or research diary can have:

- a systematic and regularly kept record of events, dates and people;
- an interpretative, self-evaluative account of the researcher's personal experiences, thoughts and feelings, with a view to trying to understand her own actions;
- a useful way of dumping painful experiences;
- a reflective account where the researcher can tease out interpretations;
- an analytic tool where data can be examined and analysed.

Journals may be set to a particular structure. Kolb's (1984) experiential learning cycle is a useful structure, whereby experience, reflection, conceptualization and experimentation form useful headings (McMullan and Cahoon, 1979; Coghlan, 1993). This format works well. You may learn to attend to details of a situation and with practice can isolate critical incidents which have affected your reactions to events and your judgement as to what to say or do. You develop skills of awareness and introspection. You are challenged in your use of theory, and learn to use theory in a practical manner. You learn to experience learning as a continuous life task as you apply your learning to future situations.

Another useful framework for journal keeping is Schein's (1999a) ORJI model. ORJI (observation, reaction, judgement, intervention) focuses on what goes on inside your head and how it affects your covert behaviour. You observe (O), react emotionally to what you have observed (R), analyse, process and make judgements based on the observations and feelings (J) and you intervene in order to make something happen (I). Schein pays particular attention to the movement from observation to judgement because he believes that frequently the individual does not pay attention to the reaction stage. In his view, the individual typically denies feelings, short circuits them and moves straight to judgement and action. You may react to an event by saying to yourself 'That's stupid' – a judgement. What you have probably done is to miss an emotional reaction of feeling threatened by the event. You may not have recognized or acknowledged that feeling of being threatened, yet it is present and is governing your judgement. By identifying and attending to feelings, (a) as initial reactions and (b) as influencing judgements, you may learn to deal with them and choose whether or not to act on them. Denial of feelings frequently means acting on them without adverting to the fact that you are acting on them. Acknowledgement of feelings to yourself and the subsequent judgement as to the origins and validity of those feelings are critical to learning and change. A journal may be structured around the four ORJI activities.

Schein's ORJI model adds a sophistication to the experiential learning cycle in two ways (Coghlan, 1993). First, it focused on a neglected area, namely the spontaneous reaction (which is typically bypassed) to an incident. It provides a framework whereby you may learn to recognize feelings and distinguish them from cognitive processes. Second, it inserts a structured reflection process that works back from action to judgement to reaction to observation. When your view of a situation is not confirmed by how events develop, you may question the original judgement. When you find that the judgement is based on an emotional reaction, then you may question the source of that reaction. With practice you may learn to become more aware of emotional reactions so as to be able to recognize them as they arise, rather than in retrospect. We provide two examples of journalling formats at the end of the chapter.

Action research skills

Second-person research involves core skills at engaging with others in the inquiry process. In his articulation of the dynamics of helping, Schein (1999a) describes several types of inquiry. His first category is what he calls *pure inquiry*. This is where the helper/consultant prompts the elicitation of the story of what is taking place and listens carefully and neutrally. She asks, 'What is going on?' 'Tell me what happened.' The second type of inquiry is what Schein calls *exploratory diagnostic inquiry*, in which the helper/consultant begins to manage the process of how the content is analysed by the other by exploring: (a) emotional processes; (b) reasoning; (c) actions. So the helper/consultant may ask, 'How do you feel about this?' 'Why do you think this happened?' 'What did you do?' 'What are you going to do?' and so on. The third type of inquiry is what Schein calls *confrontive inquiry*. This is where the helper/consultant, by sharing his or her own ideas, challenges the other to think from a new perspective. These ideas may refer to (a) process and (b) content. Examples of confrontive questions would be, 'Have you thought about doing this?' 'Have you considered that . . . might be a solution?'

Schein's typology of helper/consultant inquiry provides a useful framework for the action researcher. As the action research works at second-person research, being skilled at a collaborative approach to problem solving and change management is paramount.

Because as insider researcher you are part of the situation, you may not always act as an external consultant might, that is, be solely the enabler of emergent information and action. Of necessity you have a view of things as they are and what needs to change, and be expected to share and argue that view. Accordingly, a critical skill for you as the insider action researcher is to be able to combine advocacy with inquiry, that is to present your own inferences, attributions, opinions and viewpoints as open to testing and critique (Argyris et al., 1985; Ross and Roberts, 1994). This involves illustrating inferences with relatively directly observable data and making reasoning explicit and publicly testable in the service of learning.

Argyris and colleagues (1985: 258–261) provide seven rules for hypothesis testing:

1   Combine advocacy with inquiry.
2   Illustrate your inferences with directly observable data.
3   Make your reasoning explicit and publicly test for agreement at each inferential step.
4   Actively seek disconfirming data and alternative explanations.
5   Affirm the making of mistakes in the service of learning.
6   Actively inquire into your own impact in the learning context.
7   Design ongoing experiments to test competing views.

Torbert (1999; Fisher et al., 2000) suggests four 'parts of speech' as useful to the action inquiry role:

1   *Framing*: explicitly stating the purpose of speaking for the present occasion – what dilemma you are trying to resolve, sharing assumptions about the situation.
2   *Advocating*: explicitly stating the goal to be achieved, asserting an option, perception, feeling or proposal for action.
3   *Illustrating*: telling a bit of the concrete story that makes the advocacy concrete and orients the others more clearly.
4   *Inquiring*: questioning others to understand their perspectives and views.

Putnam (1991) asks if there are recipes which might be useful in helping others explore their reasoning processes. He suggests that questions like, 'What prevents you from . . .?' and 'What have I said or done that leads you to believe that . . .?' facilitates a focus on directly observable behaviour rather than on attribution, inference or privately held diagnosis. These interventions may occur in one-to-one or group situations.

Conclusions

In this chapter we have placed the focus on you as the action researcher. When you engage in the action research cycles of diagnosing, planning action, taking action and evaluating action with others and try to understand and shape what is going on, you are engaging in your own learning cycle activities of experiencing, reflecting, interpreting and taking action (see Figure 3.3).

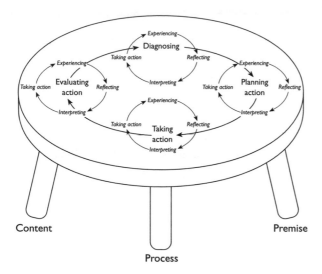

FIGURE 3.3 **COMPLEX DYNAMICS OF ACTION RESEARCH**

The underlying assumption is that you as the researcher are yourself an instrument in the generation of data. When you inquire into what is going on, when you show people your train of thought and put forward hypotheses to be tested, you are generating data. Accordingly, some of your core skills are in the areas of self-awareness and sensitivity to what you think and feel within yourself and to what you observe going on around you, supported by the conceptual analytic frameworks on which you base your observations and interpretations. In this respect your knowledge base in the field of organization behaviour on which you base your clinical observations is central. In programmes which work from an action research approach, it is likely to be critical that explicit training and education be provided to enable action researchers to develop key interpersonal inquiry and helping skills.

Exercise 3.1
Keeping a journal

EXERCISE A

Based on Kolb's (1984) experiential learning cycle (McMullan and Cahoon, 1979; Coghlan, 1993).

1 *Concrete experience*: Describe a concrete event which has taken place in the work situation – what happened, who said/did what, what you felt/said/did, what happened next, what the consequences were. Stick to a single event bounded by time. Be clinically neutral in the description – like a news bulletin.

2 *Reflection*: Now looking back with hindsight – what are your feelings/reactions/observations/judgements on this event? Perhaps now you notice that this has happened before/often. Maybe you are disappointed/angry/pleased with your own reactions at the time. How do you view your reactions/behaviour? What were the triggers that provoked your reaction?

3 *Conceptualization*: Relate relevant concepts to the experience described and formulate tentative conclusions/generalizations/hypotheses.

4 *Experimentation*: Suggest action implications for applying/testing/extending what you have reflected on, with a view to setting some behavioural goals for similar future situations. These are not general resolutions, but specific and concrete actions coming directly from your experience, reflection and conceptualization.

EXERCISE B

Based on Schein's ORJI (Schein, 1999a; Coghlan, 1993).

1 Take a situation/event where your own behaviour resulted in an unpredicted outcome.

2 Reconstruct the observation you made prior to your intervention, the emotional reaction you had, the judgement you made.

3 Identify which of the emotional reaction, the judgement or intervention may have contributed to the unpredicted outcome.

Other useful approaches to journal keeping are found in Moon (1999), Fisher et al. (2000), McNiff et al. (1996), Raelin (2000).

In your learning group or with colleagues, form a triad and adapt roles A, B and C:

- A presents an issue that she is dealing with in her action research project.
- B inquires into the issue, using Schein's intervention typology.
- C observes and then facilitates reflection on the process using Schein's intervention typology.
- Change roles and repeat.
- Change roles and repeat.

This exercise may also be done using Argyris's seven rules for hypothesis testing or Torbert's four forms of speech. McGill and Brockbank (2004) provide many useful techniques for developing skills in working in action learning sets.

The Learning Window can be used in an action research group and aims at enabling the group to distinguish between what it knows and what it is inferring and thereby acting on the basis that it thinks it knows. Making these distinctions helps keep the group focused on data.

- Quadrant 1: What the group knows has to contain solid data that have been tested and meets with consensual agreement among group members.
- Quadrant 2: What the group thinks it knows catches the inferences and attributions that group members are making and challenges the group to make those inferences explicit, to locate them in directly observable behaviour through the ladder of inference and to see them as hypotheses to be tested, rather than accepting them as facts.
- Quadrant 3: Identifies the gaps in knowledge that the group knows it needs to address and opens up an agenda for further data collection and hypothesis testing in action.

cont.

What we know	What we think we know
What we know we don't know	

[The Learning Window is an adaptation of the famous JOHARI Window and is created by Lyle Yorks, Teachers College, Columbia University, New York. We are grateful to Lyle for permission to use it.]

Part II
Issues and Challenges in Researching Your own Organization

4 Researching Your Own Organization

Doing action research in and on your own organization is a complex process and has its distinctive elements. In this chapter we outline four different forms which insider research can take, depending on the system's and your own explicit commitment to learning in action.

Researching your own organization involves undertaking research in and on your own organization while a 'complete member' (Adler and Adler, 1987). As 'permanent' is a term increasingly less applicable to today's workplace, we are using 'complete member' to refer to being a full member of your organization and wanting to remain a member within their desired career path when the research is completed.

The 'complete member role', as outlined by Adler and Adler (1987) is closest to researchers studying their own organization. Such researchers have an opportunity to acquire 'understanding in use', rather than 'reconstructed understanding'. Riemer (1977) argues that rather than neglecting 'at hand' knowledge or expertise, researchers should turn familiar situations, timely events and/or special expertise into objects of study. This orientation was partly abandoned by ethnographers during the 'classical era', when participant observation replaced the life history and the emphasis shifted towards greater objectivity and detachment. Participation and, for some, the research process involved becoming a temporary member of the organization in order to observe at first hand how life was lived, was accepted and accorded legitimacy, but subjectivity, involvement and commitment were thrust aside. What is central to this book is how complete members may undertake action research in and on their own organizations.

The focus of the researcher and system

Doing action research in your own organization is opportunistic, that is, you may be selecting an issue for research which is occurring anyway, irrespective of whether or not your inquiry takes place. We have described these as the 'core' action research project and the 'thesis' action research project (Zuber-Skerritt and Perry, 2002). Hence, we need to distinguish between the two projects, as respective responsibilities may differ. For instance, we know of a case of insider action research in which the researcher is, in effect, doing action research on a major project for which she is responsible. In this case, her academic supervisor has challenged her to differentiate between the actions of the project and the quality of her inquiry into how that project progresses and what knowledge can be extrapolated. Her research is evaluated on the quality and rigour of her inquiry, rather than on the extent and success of the organizational project that she manages and for which she is accountable to her organizational superiors. In contrast, we know of another case in which the insider researcher is working as an internal facilitator in a change project, but is not responsible for its overall management, a role assigned to a senior project manager.

Accordingly, we need to differentiate between the researcher and the system in and on which the action research is taking place, whether that system be a large organization, a community, a department or unit. We can reflect on the intended goals of both the researcher and the system. As we reflect on cases we know of insider-research projects, we notice that the focus of the researcher and system can vary. For instance, we know of an individual manager whose masters action research project was about the organizational change he was leading. His second-person intervention work to manage the politics, power dynamics and the conflicts between key protagonists was central to both his managerial role in leading change in his organization and his action research dissertation. His reflection in action was central to his dissertation. At the same time, the members of his organization had little consciousness of the fact that he was doing a dissertation for a postgraduate degree; in their eyes he was simply doing his job. We know of another case of an individual, in the same masters programme, who studied how his organization managed information. In this case, the individual's research focused on what was happening around him and was of great interest to his superiors and other members of the organization, but it did not involve him in any form of deliberate self-reflection in action.

Given that there can be a range of foci on the part of both the researcher and system, can these foci be captured in a useful way? We understand that research can be viewed along a continuum which reflects the intended focus of the research for both researcher and system (see Figure 4.1). We are distinguishing a commitment to intended self-study in action by either or both researcher and system from no such commitment.

RESEARCHER

**No intended self-study
in action**

I Traditional research approaches: collection of survey data ethnography case study	2 Pragmatic action research: internal consulting action learning

SYSTEM   **No intended self-study in action** ——————|—————— **Intended self-study in action**

3 Individual engaged in reflective study of professional practice	4 Large-scale transformational change

**Intended self-study
in action**

FIGURE 4.1 **FOCUS OF RESEARCHER AND SYSTEM**

Quadrant 1

Quadrant 1 is defined by the absence of intended self-study in action by both researcher and system. There is study but it is not deliberately in-action. This is a situation where the researcher is focusing on a perspective, issue or problem within the system as if external to himself/herself, and is not engaging in any deliberate self-reflection in-action as part of the research process (Anderson et al., 1994; Flyvbjerg, 2001). At the same time, the system itself is not committed to engaging in any intended self-study in-action. The researcher may be researching patterns of statistical information, customer preferences, or writing a case history around a particular strategic initiative or a period of time. For the researcher, these are data which are gathered and analysed using established methodologies.

Alvesson (1999) addresses the situation of doing ethnographical research in one's own organization. He calls it 'self-ethnography', rather than insider ethnography or home culture ethnography. 'Self-ethnography' involves studying a setting in which the researcher is a participant on more or less equal terms with other participants. Participation comes first and is only occasionally complemented by research-focused observation and hence 'observing participant' is a more appropriate term than 'participant observer'. The self-ethnographer relies on familiarity with the setting as the empirical starting point. If you are an insider researcher working within the ethnography tradition, you have to work hard at liberating yourself from subjectivity in order to meet the intellectual requirements of this research tradition. Young (1991) provides a good case of doing ethnography in his own organization. He reports how there was a culture of secrecy within the police force of which he was a member. Social science research was equated with 'claptrap' and anyone engaged in it ran the risk of being labelled a traitor and his or her promotion would be put in jeopardy. Therefore, he had to undertake his study surreptitiously and he refers to his work as 'writing espionage'.

The ethnographic role and the action researcher role are closely interconnected and sharply distinguished (Schein, 1987). The ethnographic observer attempts to be an unobtrusive observer of the inner life of an organization, while the action researcher works at enabling obtrusive change. Since the self-ethnography approach is not the subject of this book, we are not including any further exploration of this quadrant. In terms of the focus of this book, we are addressing research projects which are contained in Quadrants 2, 3 and 4.

Quadrant 2

Quadrant 2 applies where there is no intended self-study in action on the part of the researcher, while what is being studied is the system in-action. We see this as 'pragmatic' action research, which comprises management action, internal consulting projects and some action learning (Coghlan and Casey, 2001; Coghlan and McAuliffe, 2003; Coghlan et al., 2004). Coghlan (2003) refers to this as 'mechanistic-oriented' action research by which he means that the research is framed in terms of managing change or solving a problem; it is directed at confronting and resolving a pre-identified issue.

There are many examples of Quadrant 2 insider action research. Coghlan and colleagues (2004) provide a broad range of cases in which managers engaged in action research on particular issues confronting their companies: improving influence and performance in a multinational subsidiary; building inter-organizational relationships in a global virtual community; implementing a 360-degree feedback programme; managing human resources, among others. Bartunek and colleagues (2000) also present three case examples of such research. Three of the authors, acting in their organizational managerial capacity, carried out action research projects in their own organizations – in a bank, a manufacturing company and a public utility respectively. The research projects were oriented towards improving operational action, and there is no reported self-study in-action on the part of the authors. Frohman (1997) and Friedman (2001b) present situations where individuals, typically middle to lower order rank, took initiatives to make changes in their organizations.

There is a broad range of accounts of Quadrant 2 action research in nursing. Examples of action research in the clinical area illustrate interventions to improve: pain management (Simons, 2002); stroke care (Gibbon and Little, 1995); palliative care (Cooper and Hewison, 2002); breast cancer care (Lauri and Sainio, 1998); psychiatric and emergency services (Heslop et al., 2000). Examples of action research in the organizational and operational areas include: care plan planning and audit (McElroy et al., 1995; Webb and Pontin, 1997); continuous quality improvement (Potter et al., 1994); clinical teaching (Hyrkas, 1997); introducing clinical practice facilitators (Kelly and Simpson, 2001); and health visiting parenting programme (Kilgour and Fleming, 2000).

Action research in Quadrant 2 is typically the type of research undertaken in MBA programmes, where the focus is manager-led operational projects within a limited, specified time frame. These may well be projects already underway in an organization, and accordingly are opportunistically adopted by manager-MBA students as their action research project. Clearly, such opportunistic adoption is not confined to MBA situations, but may be undertaken by teachers, nurses, social workers, clinicians and like situations where course participants choose pre-existing projects for their own research topic. In these situations, action researchers attempt to bring the action research cycles of inquiry to a project which has not been set up as an action research project. This may make severe demands on action researchers' ability to manage organizational politics. Depending on the origin and scope of the project within this quadrant, the internal researcher may be working with an external consultant who has been hired to facilitate the change.

From their three case experiences of manager-led action research projects, Bartunek and colleagues (2000) generalize a number of relevant issues and themes:

1   The initial assignment to carry out work that leads to the action research project is likely to come from the manager's superiors and to be part of the manager's job description.
2   The other participants in the intervention are likely to be subordinates who need to buy-in to the change project.
3   The intervention is likely to be aimed at increased productivity.
4   Managers may find it helpful to constitute a consulting team to assist in the intervention.
5   Data gathering can take place through a variety of formal and informal means.
6   Feedback sessions can be integrated into the work day or conducted separately.
7   The manager is likely to have a personal stake in the outcome of the intervention.

8   The managers were all receiving training in action research while carrying out their interventions.

Quadrant 3

Quadrant 3 applies where the researcher is engaged in an intended self-study of herself in action, but the system is not. The researcher may be engaging in a study to improve professional practice. She is engaging simultaneously in a process of self-reflection and examining her own assumptions in action and learning about herself as events unfold. The researcher becomes a 'reflective practitioner' (Schon, 1983). Coghlan (2003) refers to this as 'organistic-oriented' action research where the inquiry process is a value in itself. In organistic-oriented action research researchers engage in an action inquiry process in which inquiry into their own assumptions and ways of thinking and acting is central to the research process. As mentioned earlier, Judi Marshall (1999, 2001) describes this first-person research/practice in terms of: (a) inquiring into the inner and outer arcs of attention; (b) engaging in cycles of action and reflection; and (c) being active and receptive.

Krim (1988) provides a case example of Quadrant 3 action research. He provides a dramatic account of an action inquiry project in action. He outlines the context of change in a city hall power culture, and describes both the political and conflictual dynamics within that culture and the processes of his own personal learning (see Box 4.1).

Krim (1988) reports how he, as initiator and coordinator of a new labour-management cooperation programme based on employee participation in a city hall, sought to use himself as the key learning strategy, whereby his management style would be central to the inquiry process. He outlines the context of change in a city hall power culture, and describes both the political and conflictual dynamics within that culture and the processes of his own personal learning. He describes his reflection process in terms of a pyramid of five steps:

Box 4.1 Action research in Quadrant 3

- recording and observing on a daily and hourly basis;
- a weekly selection and analysis of critical incidents;

cont.

- an exploration of these issues with his academic supervisor;
- rehearsal and role playing with his supervisor in anticipation of further critical incidents,
- a public testing in the real life situation.

He reports how this cycle of continuous rehearsal and performance allowed him to improve his performance in highly political and conflictual situations. From this process he received feedback on his management style, particularly how he tended to 'de-authorize' himself, and so he adopted some practical rules of thumb to help him develop new behaviours. He reports how he was accused of spying as his research notes were pilfered from his computer and circulated among his antagonists.

This case provides a useful example of Quadrant 3 research as it focuses on how Krim's own personal learning in action was integral to the study.

A Quadrant 3 research may be preselected or it may emerge. Where the research agenda is self-selected by the researcher it may focus on the researcher's job or role within the organization. It may be that the Quadrant 3 research emerges out of a Quadrant 2 project. Meehan and Coghlan (forthcoming) provide such an example (see Box 4.2).

Meehan and Coghlan (forthcoming) describe a case in which Meehan, in his organizational role, was asked by his superior to evaluate the addiction counselling service in his regional health area. The service was primarily treatment focused and provided a service to help those with addiction problems end their dependence on mood-altering substances and to rebuild their relationships with their families, friends and colleagues.	**Box 4.2 Action research from Quadrant 2 to Quadrant 3**

Meehan met the group of counsellors. As the group explored the issue

cont.

of evaluation, resistance emerged. There was concern that no matter how good the evaluation was the organization would not accept it. The feeling of alienation that the group felt was surfacing with an air of futility about the process being articulated. At this time Meehan found himself actively listening to the group and he speculated that if an effective evaluation was to take place the feelings of the participants needed to be heard and dealt with in some way. He was becoming aware that he was utilizing listening and counselling skills in the process. The counselling skills were skills he had learned as a clinical psychiatric nurse and it enabled the group to explore feelings they had about these issues. As time went on he became more convinced that he was working on a project that would really benefit from an action research approach and he entered into discussions with the group on the issue. His thinking in this regard was that the action research approach would be likely to produce insights that could not be gleaned in other ways. He hoped that the process would enable the group to get new and innovative insights into the service and to take action based on them

Traditional research methods would not yield insights into the organizational difficulties that impede progress within the service. Action research would also enable the group to meet its objective of taking action based on the process of exploring and making sense of the issues, in order to carry out an evaluation of the addiction counselling service.

Meehan introduced the group to the notion of cooperative inquiry and the group agreed to pursue the issues pertaining to themselves and the service in that mode of reflection on experience through a cooperative inquiry group process. Over a six-month period the group met eleven times and explored three themes: feelings of alienation and powerlessness; the lack of strategic direction in the service; and professional identity and autonomy. They carried out a SWOT (**s**trengths, **w**eaknesses, **o**pportunities and **t**hreats) analysis of the service and identified areas for change, both within themselves and in the management of the service.

As he led the group through the formulation of an action plan to initiate a service evaluation, Meehan found himself confronted by a feeling of futility within the group. On one level he was getting feedback that his intervention was helpful but how it was helpful was not articulated. On

cont.

another level the group was sceptical about the usefulness of the evaluation. The manager assumed that there was a feeling it was all done before and 'what's the point?' Meehan then began to see his role as a go-between or an arbitrator between the management team and the addiction counsellors and in some way he perceived that if he could get a good evaluation of the process utilizing management input, addiction counselling input and from a service users' perspective that would solve the issue. However, intuitively he was picking up resistance and vibes saying that this was not going to work.

The group of addiction counsellors worked in the group to reflect on their experience and to develop new and creative ways of looking at things. They also learned how to act to change things they wanted to change and explored how to do things better. Each member acted as a co-subject in the reflection phases and a co-researcher in the action phases. They enacted the action research cycles of reflection and action in a psychologically safe environment, which enabled them to make sense of their experience and take steps to initiate change. Overall the outcomes of the cooperative inquiry process were that there was a reduction in the feelings of alienation and powerlessness in the group and this was evidenced in the enthusiasm with which the group subsequently engaged in the evaluation. There grew a commitment to work in partnership with all stakeholders and service users in evaluation and developing the service. The group was beginning to look at issues from other perspectives and this appeared to reduce hostility and fear. There were also real issues about their power in the organization – at one level they felt victims in the process, yet it was obvious that unless they agreed with changes they were unlikely to be implemented.

Meehan found the whole process difficult yet rewarding. It was an ongoing dynamic and he found he learned a lot in the process. It was the first time he had consciously bridged the gap between his role as a clinician and as a manager. It showed him how to utilize his skills as a clinician in management. He found the action research cycles to be very useful and it produced insights, which he believed could not be gleaned in other ways. The process was also a healing one and he believed it empowered the group to deal with underlying difficulties in the service.

Through this process Meehan believed he got insights into how he could further develop as a manager and a person. One particular change

cont.

in his behaviour and role as a manager that occurred in this process was how he now perceived his role differently. Traditionally he had viewed his role as an agent of control; now he viewed himself in a different way. The process enabled him to explore new and interesting ways of viewing his role as a manager; it gave him an insight into potential ways of working with alienation and powerlessness in the workplace. Hitherto he functioned as what Frost and Robinson (1999) described as a 'toxic handler', which he now viewed as an unhealthy way of managing organizational pain. He now saw one of his managerial roles as that of healer (Quick et al., 1996).

In hindsight he was able to manage many of the political elements because as an insider he understood the process politics of the organization. He found himself as a middle manager who has to understand internal and external pressures on the organization and satisfy the personal or competing interests. The personal and emotional issues remained confidential to the group but the broader learning from the group was discussed. Changes to the management structures, issues regarding supervision, renegotiations regarding time frames for completion were all dealt with well and there was no conflict on these issues.

Quadrant 4

Quadrant 4 is where both the researcher and the system are engaged in intended study in action. The system has made or is making a commitment to change. For example, the system may undertake a system-wide transformational change programme in which everything in the system is open to review, as instanced in the movement to quality of working life (QWL), business process re-engineering and organization development projects or any of those through a learning history approach. In this instance, there is a broad commitment to reflecting on experience and learning. The researcher's role involves being part of this collective reflection and learning, and articulating what is happening. There is active participation by both the system and the individual. In a large-scale system change project, it is likely that there are external consultants, hence the need for insider–outsider collaboration (Titchen and Binnie, 1993; Bartunek and Louis, 1996; de Guerre, 2002; Adler et al., 2004). Aspirations to form communities of inquiry in organizations would be located in this quadrant (see Box 4.3).

The case of OilCo provides an interesting picture of a large-scale corporate transformation (Kleiner and Roth, 2000). Presented through the approach of the learning history, the story of how the company worked through its transformation is told both in narrative form and through a number of themes, such as the quest for financial literacy, leadership, governance and identity, among others. What is interesting about the learning history approach is that the case is described through the perspectives of the multiple participants and stakeholders in what Kleiner and Roth call a 'jointly told tale'. The accounts of the participants are juxtaposed with comments from the authors as 'learning historians' and the readers are invited, not only to reflect on what they are reading and apply it to their own experience, but to do so in discussion groups with other managers and colleagues. Hence the story of the company becomes an intervention into the thought processes and practice of the readers as well as into the members of the company who read and discuss their own history.

Box 4.3 Action research in Quadrant 4

Kleiner and Roth (2000) provided a learning history account of an oil company in which the new chief executive officer (CEO) set the company on a deliberate course of learning and transformation. The change agenda was initiated through an economic model and then moved to issues of governance, structures, relationships, communication and basic attitudes and behaviour. Fundamental identity and ways of thinking, feeling and acting changed over time. The learning history provides both the observations and reflections on what happened by the participants and the 'analytic' comments by the external learning historians. In the learning history, participants at all hierarchical levels show their perceptions and experiences of what took place.

The juxtaposition of multiple views with the view of the learning historians provides a challenging opportunity for the readers and those to whom the learning history is disseminated, particularly the members of the company, to reflect on how the case challenges them to think about their own reasoning processes. A parallel case in a car company is described in Roth and Kleiner (2000).

The research process itself may provoke a move from one quadrant to another. An action researcher, operating in Quadrant 2 for instance, may find that the technical problem being researched is a symptom of underlying cultural assumptions, and so its resolution carries more far reaching implications than was envisaged at the outset. The dimensions of research in Quadrant 3 may evolve into Quadrant 4. It may be that the researcher's personal development through the research process involves a gradual movement from Quadrant 2 to 3. Participants in the masters programme in Management Practice at the Irish Management Institute-University of Dublin, which is a part-time action research oriented programme, reported that they perceived the two-year programme as a journey from Quadrant 2 to 3, with Quadrant 4 the desired outcome in the long term.

The grid acts as a mechanism for subject selection. You may select a subject, based on: (a) a desired outcome for yourself and/or your system; (b) the opportunity or access to areas of the organization; and (c) your sense of your possession of the level of skill required to work in any particular quadrant. You may ask yourself: What quadrant am I in? What quadrant do I think I am in? Which quadrant am I best at? Quadrant 4 is clearly the most difficult and demanding in terms of conceptual, analytic and practical knowledge and skill.

Action research at home

Not all action research in your own organization is done at places of work. Box 4.4 illustrates action research at home.

Goode and Bartunek (1990) reflect on this case in terms of two issues. First, this case is an example of action research in an underbounded system. As this subject is not central to the theme of this book we will not reflect further on this point. Second, and the one which concerns us in the context of action research in your own organization, is how the action researcher initiated research in an organization where she had a personal stake. Goode and Bartunek point to two roles the action researcher played. One role was that of a long-term participant in the system, which meant she shared the concerns of the fellow residents and had credibility. The other role was a short-term consultant role where her knowledge of action research provided guidance for the process. She was willing to take an educative, directive and participative approach to enable the resolution of problems and the emergence of new structures.

Goode and Bartunek (1990) describe a self-initiated action research project in an apartment complex, where Goode initiated a process to address a problem of direct personal concern. In the apartment complex where Goode was a resident, there were problems relating to mail delivery and security. Single efforts to address resident concerns had been unsuccessful. Goode approached several concerned residents, discussed the problem with them and explained action research in order to foster an environment which enabled collaboration and the search for multiple causes of the problem, rather than the unitary blaming of the complex's caretakers, which was common. Goode then formulated a plan for gathering information, which involved: (1) producing an informational letter which she distributed to all residents; (2) conducting preliminary meetings with some of the residents and the caretakers; (3) conducting an informational session with anyone interested in participating; and (4) interviewing all interested individuals. All these actions took place and the data generated was analysed under such headings as: organization strengths, existing mail security problems and existing group-level structures and problems. A feedback session was held at which task forces were formed to address particular issues and actions implemented.

**Box 4.4
Action
research at
home**

Conclusions

In this chapter we have reflected on the subject of doing research in and on your own organization. Researching your own organization involves undertaking research in and on your own organization while a complete member, which in this context means wanting to remain a member within your desired career path when the research is completed. In undertaking action research in and on your own organization, the commitment to learning in action by both the system and yourself is a useful defining construct. If the research project is accompanied by the system's commitment to learning in action, then secondary access is easier. If your organizational role is that of internal consultant, then your research role is integral to that role. If on the other hand you are a manager, then you are taking on the researcher role in addition, which may create confusion.

As an insider action researcher you are engaged in first-person research, using your preunderstanding of organizational knowledge and organizational studies for your own personal and professional development. You are engaging in second-person research by working on practical issues of concern to your organization in collaboration with colleagues and relevant others. You are engaging in third-person research by generating understanding and theory which is extrapolated from the experience.

Doing action research in your own organization involves: (a) clarifying the action research project in terms of both your own and the system's commitment to learning in action; and (b) managing issues of role and secondary access.

5

Preunderstanding, Role Duality and Access

The dynamics of doing action research in your own organization in Quadrants 2, 3 and 4 involve building on the insider knowledge you have already (preunderstanding) and managing the two roles you have (your standard organizational roles and now in addition the action researcher role) and negotiating access. We now explore these.

Preunderstanding

According to Gummesson, 'preunderstanding refers to such things as people's knowledge, insights and experience before they engage in a research programme' (2000: 57). The knowledge, insights and experience of the insider action researcher apply, not only to theoretical understanding of organizational dynamics, but also to the lived experience of your own organization. Some misunderstand the notion of preunderstanding and equate it with tacit knowledge. Preunderstanding includes both explicit and tacit knowledge. Personal experience and knowledge of your own system and job is a distinctive preunderstanding for the insider action researcher.

One advantage you have as an insider-researcher over an outsider-researcher is that you have valuable knowledge about the cultures and informal structures of your organization. Organizations lead two lives. The formal or public life is presented in terms of its formal documentation – mission statement, goals, assets, resources, annual reports, organizational chart, and so on. The informal or private life is experiential, that is, it is the life as experienced by its members – its cultures, norms, traditions, power blocs, and so on. In their informal lives, organizations are centres of love, hate, envy, jealousy, good and ill will, politics, infighting, cliques, political factions and so on, a stark contrast to the formal rational image organizations tend to portray. You have valuable experience of this, though you don't know it all. While this knowledge is an advantage, it is also a disadvantage as you are likely to be part of the organization's culture and find it difficult to stand back from it in order to assess and critique it. You may need to be in tune with your own feelings as an organizational member – where your feelings of good will are directed, where your frustrations are and so on.

Nielsen and Repstad (1993) outline some examples of such experience and preunderstanding. You have knowledge of your organization's everyday life. You know the everyday jargon. You know the legitimate and taboo phenomena of what can be talked about and what cannot. You know what occupies colleagues' minds. You know how the informal organization works and whom to turn to for information and gossip. You know the critical events and what they mean within the organization. You are able to see beyond objectives which are merely window dressing. When you are inquiring you can use the internal jargon and draw on your own experience in asking questions and interviewing, and be able to follow up on replies and so obtain richer data. You are able to participate in discussions or merely observe what is going on without others being necessarily aware of your presence. You can participate freely without drawing attention to yourself and creating suspicion.

There are also some disadvantages to be being close to the data. When you are interviewing you may assume too much and so not probe as much as if you were an outsider or ignorant of the situation. You may think you know the answer and not expose your current thinking to alternative reframing. In insider research epistemic reflexivity is the constant analysis of your lived experience as well as your own theoretical and methodological presuppositions. This helps you to retain an awareness of the importance of other people's definitions and understandings of theirs. You may find it difficult to obtain relevant data, because as a member you have to cross departmental, functional or hierarchical lines or because as an insider you may be denied deeper access, which might not be denied an outsider. Ferguson and Ferguson (2001) caution against insider action researchers believing that they fully understand their own contexts, when in fact their perspectives are only partial. The moral, in their view, is to be honest about your perspectives from which you operate and be open to disconfirming evidence – perhaps seeking it out through interviews.

Coghlan's (1996) preunderstanding was based on three elements. First, there was his membership of the organization and basic familiarity with its members, ideology, values, culture, ministries and language or terminology. Second, there was his experience as a member of the region's central administrative team in which he worked as an internal organization development consultant in projects of strategy and change. Through this element, he was personally familiar with many of the interventions, and the reports and files pertaining to those interventions. Third, his education, training and experience in organization development provided a familiarity with the constructs for reflecting on and conceptualizing change processes. Political knowledge was a critical element of preunderstanding in Krim's (1988) city hall organization. However, as he points out, his understanding of the informal knowledge-based power structure was inadequate when he underestimated the connection power of one particular individual whom he tried to replace. That person was able to muster considerable support to resist Krim's efforts to replace her and severe confrontational conflict ensued.

Schein (1992, 1999b) describes organizational culture as patterns of basic assumptions which have been passed on through generations of organizational members and which are unnoticed and taken for granted. Accordingly, the approach to uncovering cultural assumptions is a dialogue between organizational members and an external process consultant who facilitates the exploration of what assumptions underlie artefacts and values. As an insider-researcher you may need an external consultant to help you make sense of your experience. The academic supervisor may play this role. Krim (1988) reported how, in his meetings with his academic supervisor, he would role play critical incidents. These role plays were important in his reflective learning process.

Gorinski and Ferguson (1997) share a conversation about their respective experiences of being an insider action researcher. They identify positive aspects of accessibility, credibility, trustworthiness, commitment and familiarity with the research context and personnel. They found the barriers to be: communication difficulties, time limitations, power positions and how cultural openness changed as they found themselves being left out of things. Their conclusion is that they had to 'make the road by walking'.

Journalling is an important mechanism for learning to reflect on and gain insights into your preunderstanding. Through recording your experiences, thoughts and feelings over time as you move through your project you can begin to identify gaps between what you think you know and then find that you don't, or between explicit and tacit knowledge. You can begin to learn to stand back and critique what you have taken for granted hitherto. The journalling process helps your meta learning of content, process and premise in the arena of your preunderstanding, the exposure of what you know already because of your closeness to the issues and the organization with what you are discovering as you engage in first-, second- and third-person inquiry.

Role duality: organizational and researcher roles

In action research the traditional distinction between the researcher and the researched diminishes. Working in Quadrants 2, 3 and 4 of Figure 4.1 the insider action researcher role is added to the complete member role, discussed earlier.

Ashforth and colleagues (2000) explore the nature of roles. They present a number of useful constructs. Role boundary is defined as the scope of a role. Role boundaries can be flexible (that is, their boundaries can be pliable spatially and temporally) and they can be permeable (one can be physically in one role and psychologically and/or behaviourally in another). For Ashforth et al. these constructs of role flexibility and permeability enable transition from one role to another. In terms of doing action research in your own organization, you may be in your office or at a meeting in your organization exercising your organizational role (physical and spatial) and at the same time, probing for answers to questions in your research role.

Ashforth et al. also explore the notion of role identity; that is, how a role cues specific goals, values, behaviours and so on. Role identities are socially constructed definitions of self-in-role, consisting of contrasts between core and peripheral features. In Ashforth et al's. view, combining the construct of role boundary in terms of flexibility and permeability with that of role identity in terms of contrast between core and peripheral features can be arranged along a continuum from high role segmentation to high role integration. Roth and colleagues (2004) apply Ashforth et al.'s framework to three case examples of insider action research as insider action researchers span boundaries as they enact roles in both the organizational setting and the academic setting. For example, they apply frames of reference from the academic setting to the organizational setting. They also note that role duality may change character between high segmentation and high integration as the project progresses.

Augmenting your normal organizational membership role with the research enterprise can be difficult and awkward, and can become confusing and overwhelming. As a result, in trying to sustain a full organizational membership role and the research perspective simultaneously, you are likely to encounter role conflict. Your organizational role may demand total involvement and active commitment, while the research role may demand a more detached, more theoretic, objective and neutral observer position. This conflict may lead you to experience role detachment, where you begin to feel as an outsider in both roles (Adler and Adler, 1987).

Your organizational relationships are typically lodged and enmeshed in a network of membership affiliations, as you have been and continue to be a participant in the organization. These friendships and research ties can vary in character from openness to restrictiveness. You are likely to find that your associations with various individuals or groups in the setting will influence your relations with others whom you encounter, affecting the character of the data you can gather from them.

Your organizational role or roles will influence the degree of role confusion or ambiguity that you experience as an insider action researcher and your ability to cope with your situation. If your sole job in your organization is that of internal change consultant, then you are already a researcher in your own organization. We see this as a single role with low potential for role confusion. Quadrants 2 and 4 of Figure 4.1 incorporate such internal researchers. On the other hand, if your job is that of manager, then you are taking on a researcher's role in addition to your managerial job. Hence you have to manage dual roles – manager and researcher – and there is high potential for role confusion. Quadrant 3 of Figure 4.1 is a good example of this situation. Single-role researchers whose job involves research type activities are quite distinct from dual-role researchers where research activity is a separate role from their standard functional role. In terms of the cases we discuss throughout the book, we can see that Krim (1988) is an example of a dual-role researcher whereas Coghlan (1996) is an example of a single-role researcher.

Pace and Argona (1991) provide an account of an eight-year participatory action research programme in Xerox in which management and trade unions worked together to implement a quality of working life programme. As internal consultants, the authors found themselves in multiple roles: human resource strategists, applied researchers, process champions and interfacers with corporate office, all roles which had to be integrated and consequently were transparent to management and unions as partners of the project.

Feelings of detachment can be oriented towards one or other of these roles and increase or decrease as the research progresses. When you are caught between the loyalty tugs, behavioural claims and identification dilemmas you initially align yourself with your organizational role. Elizur (1999) uses the term 'self-differentiation' to review how he, as an insider consultant, managed: (a) to contain emotions and to relate to emotionally charged issues in a balanced way; and (b) to maintain his own autonomy and self-identity in these situations. Your involvement in the two roles affects your relations with organizational members (Adler and Adler, 1987). The new dimension of your relationship to members and/or your new outside interests set you apart from ordinary members.

Homa (1998) reflected on what it was like to combine the roles of CEO and researcher. He provided a number of useful pieces of potential advice:

Box 5.1 An example of dual role management

1 You need to be reasonably on top of your job as it is hard to switch psychologically from management responsibility to research without it. Therefore, selecting the right time in your career to do research is an important choice. You need to possess effective personal organization – time management and the ability to create a distance between work and study so that you can leave the organization for periods of uninterrupted study.
2 You need excellent secretarial support, particularly if you don't do your own typing.
3 Over time you need to balance the achievement of being a manager and working through others with the solitary work of a researcher.
4 You need a strong management team and a strong and supportive chairman.

Roth and colleagues (2004) recount how a conflict between the two roles arose in terms of timing. In the organizational setting there was pressure to present conclusions from the research setting, even though in research terms the insider action researcher thought it was too early and that the data had not been fully reflected on. In Roth et al.'s view, 'In doing so the insider action researcher tried to legitimize the researcher role before it was mature in that setting, giving the opposite result' (2004: 212).

Nielsen and Repstad (1993) cite a number of specific role duality related advantages and disadvantages of insider research. You may have a strong desire to influence and want to change the organization. You may feel empathy for your colleagues and so be motivated to keep up the endeavour. These are beneficial in that they may sustain your energy and be a drawback in that they may lead to erroneous conclusions. You have to deal with the dilemma of writing a report on what you have found, and dealing with the aftermath with superiors and colleagues, if you do, on the one hand, and doctoring your report to keep your job, on the other. When you are observing colleagues at work and recording your observations, you may be perceived as spying or breaking peer norms. Probably the most crucial dilemma for you as an action researcher in your own

organization, particularly when you want to remain and progress in the organization is managing organizational politics. We return to this subject in
Chapter 7.

A practical issue you have to deal with is that you may be too close to the
issues and the people in the organization and so you have to work more consciously and explicitly at the process of inquiry. If you have been trained in a
particular discipline or are familiar with a particular function you may not be
open to seeing problems from other perspectives. You may be too close to the
people and the situations you are researching. What if the research involves cri-
tiquing your friends or close colleagues? It may be difficult for you to stand back
from the situation and question your own assumptions, which heretofore have
been unquestioned. Epistemic reflexivity correctly enacted incorporates challenging presuppositions derived from closeness to people and issues.

Coghlan (1996) interviewed the executive leaders who had formed and led
particular parts of the change processes. When he was interviewing the executive with whom he had personally worked closely, Coghlan noticed that he was
contributing to the conversation more than he had done in the interviews
with the other executives. He realized that because he was so close to this particular situation he was tending to shape the outcome and so needed to build in
a balancing mechanism. Accordingly, he sent a draft of the chapter dealing
with the particular period under review to that executive and interviewed him
a second time. In this way his account and analysis of the events of the period
was amended through further dialogue with this protagonist.

Access

Primary access refers to the ability to get into the organization and be allowed
to undertake research. So as you are already a member of the organization, you
have primary access; you are already in. While you have primary access, you
may or may not have secondary access, that is, you may or may not have access
to specific parts of the organization which are relevant to your research. This is
especially true of research in Quadrant 3 where the system is not committed to
self-study in action. By parts of the organization we mean not only functional
areas such as departments, but also hierarchical areas whereby there is restricted
access to specific privileged information, which may not be available otherwise.
Insider-researchers do find, however, that membership of the organization
means that some avenues are closed to them because of their position in the
organization. Clearly, any researcher's status in the organization has an impact on
access. Access at one level may automatically lead to limits or access at other

levels. The higher the status of the researcher the more access he or she has or the more networks that are accessible, particularly downward through the hierarchy. Of course, being in a high hierarchical position may exclude access to many informal and grapevine networks. Fundamentally, secondary access means access to documentation, data, people and meetings. In relation to research in Quadrants 2 and 4, the system takes responsibility for secondary access because it is committed to self-study in action.

An important aspect of negotiating the research project is to assess the degree of secondary access to which one is allowed. Dual-role researchers may experience more problems than single-role researchers. Of course, what is espoused at the outset and then actually allowed may be different once the project is underway and at a critical stage. There may be a significant gap between the aspiration towards 'purity' of research and the reality. How access is realized may depend on the type of research being undertaken and the way information is disseminated.

Negotiating access with your superiors is a tricky business, particularly if the research project aims at good work and not something bland. It raises questions about the different needs which must be satisfied through the project. As an insider action researcher you have needs around doing a solid piece of research which will contribute to your own career and development (first-person research, for me). You also have needs around doing a piece of research in the organization which will be of benefit to the organization (second-person research, for us) and contribute to general theory for the broader academic community (third-person research, for them). Balancing these three audiences is difficult. In general, researchers' superiors have needs around confidentiality, sensitivity to others and organizational politics.

For you, the researcher, who is undertaking research as part of a degree programme or who seeks to publish, a particular issue relating to access is the fact that what is researched will be going outside the organization. Theses and dissertations are read by people external to the organization and are filed in libraries, with their abstracts disseminated to a wider audience. Bartunek and Louis (1996) see this as an 'outsider' role the insider also plays. In its extreme, organizations can be paranoid about information going outside the organization, or at least be nervous about it.

Once again we emphasize the value of journalling in exploring role duality. Role ambiguity and role conflict can challenge how your role identity is flexible and permeable. Locating yourself on the continuum between role integration and role segmentation and exploring the forces whereby you are enabled or inhibited in exercising both your organizational role and your insider action researcher role is key to first- and second-person inquiry and practice.

Coghlan (1996) undertook research on change in the region of the Roman Catholic religious order of which he is a member. He was engaging in a longitudinal study of organizational change interventions over an eighteen-year period as doctoral research. As a member he had general primary access to the events of the eighteen-year period under study. As a former member of the central administration team he had more specific access to restricted archives and files. As organization development (OD) consultant he had access to the project of reviewing the change programmes in the organization, whereby the granting of permission to access archives and files for research purposes was perceived as an extension of his OD role. At one point he sought and was granted access to more restricted archives, where he considered he needed to scan the minutes of confidential personnel meetings to find further clarification of issues found in less restricted archives.

**Box 5.2
Role
duality of
access**

Conclusions

Role duality and secondary access tend to be research project specific and organizationally dependent, whereas preunderstanding tends to be researcher specific. Therefore, preunderstanding is not directly linked to the quadrant schema presented in Figure 4.1. Preunderstanding, as the word suggests, is what the insider brings to the research process. In summary, secondary access pertains to the specific nature of the research project. In Quadrants 2 and 4 the system takes responsibility for secondary access, and it may be more readily available if all the relevant parts of the system are committed to the project. It is more problematic in Quadrant 3, where the system does not necessarily have a commitment to your action research.

6

Managing Organizational Politics and Ethics

While doing any research in an organization is very political (Punch, 1994), doing research in and on your own organization is particularly so. In this chapter, we examine the politics and ethics involved in doing action research in your own organization.

The politics of researching your own organization

Clearly any form of research in any organization has its political dynamics. Political forces can undermine research endeavours and block planned change. Gaining access, using data, disseminating and publishing reports are intensely political acts. Take for example, the act of diagnosis, which we discussed in Chapter 2 and will revisit in Chapter 10. Diagnosis is never a neutral act; it rarely affects stakeholders in the same way. Some may benefit and some may be harmed because it exposes weaknesses in performance. So while action research diagnosis is a collaborative activity, raising certain questions and applying judgements to particular issues may have severe political implications.

Therefore, doing action research in your own organization is political. Indeed it might be considered subversive. Action research has a subversive quality about it. It examines everything. It stresses listening. It emphasizes questioning. It fosters courage. It incites action. It abets reflection and it endorses democratic participation. Any or all of these characteristics may be threatening to existing organizational norms, particularly in those organizations that lean towards a hierarchical control culture. Meyerson (2001) calls those who quietly enact change in their own organizations as 'tempered radicals'. Cooklin (1999) refers to the insider change agent as the 'irreverent inmate', one who is a supporter of the people in the organization, a saboteur of the organization's rituals and a questioner of some of its beliefs. While as the action researcher you may see yourself attempting to generate valid and useful information in order to facilitate free and informed choice so that there will be commitment to those choices in accordance with the theory and practice of action research (Argyris and Schon, 1996), you may find that, as Kakabadse (1991) argues, what constitutes valid information is intensely political.

Accordingly, you need to be politically astute in engaging in action research, becoming what Buchanan and Badham (1999) call a 'political entrepreneur'. In their view, this role implies a behaviour repertoire of political strategies and tactics and a reflective self-critical perspective on how those political behaviours may be deployed. Buchanan and Boddy (1992) describe the management of the political role in terms of two activities, performing and backstaging. *Performing* involves you in the public performance role of being active in the change process, building participation for change, pursuing the change agenda rationally and logically, while backstage activity involves the recruitment and maintenance of support and the reduction of resistance. *Backstaging* comprises skills at intervening in the political and cultural systems, through justifying, influencing and negotiating, defeating opposition and so on. Because you are an insider you have a preunderstanding of the organization's power structures and politics, and are able to work in ways that are in keeping with the political conditions without compromising the project or your own career.

As you engage in your action research project, you need to be prepared to work the political system, which involves balancing the organization's formal justification of what it wants in the project with your tacit personal justification for political activity. Throughout the project you will have to maintain your credibility as an effective driver of change and as an astute political player. The key to this is assessing the power and interests of relevant stakeholders in relation to aspects of the project. One particular manager may have a great deal of influence with regard to budget allocation, but little influence with regard to strategic decision making.

Pettigrew (2003) reflects on his own role as a political entrepreneur. He notes that it can be exhilarating when it appears that your advocacy, enthusiasm and energy have created desired effects towards some defined outcomes and equal and opposite despair when things go wrong. He reflects that there is a fine line between acting in a politically astute manner and acting unethically. In his view, action researchers have to build relationships and trust with people who operate from different mental models and at different levels. Yet working as a change agent cannot always be done with openness, honesty and transparency. He judges that the real skill in the political entrepreneur is knowing that the game is everything and that it is 'theories-in-action' rather than espoused theories that count.

Managing political relationships

In order to be able to manage the content and control agendas of the action research project and the power-political processes of influencing and ensuring the legitimacy of your project, you need to be able to manage your superiors, peers and colleagues (Kotter, 1985). Building on the work of Greiner and Schein (1988), we have identified ten key power relationships (see Figure 6.1). All of the ten key power relationships need to be considered and managed when carrying out a Quadrant 3-type action research project where the system is not committed to self-study in action. The first two relationships may not be of great importance for Quadrant 2 and 4 research projects where the system is committed to self-study in action.

First, there is your relationship with your sponsor. It is most likely, if you have a middle or low organizational rank, that you have a sponsor who provides permission and primary access to undertake the research, both in the initial and latter stages of the project. Where the research is part of a degree programme, the sponsor grants you permission to have time off to attend the course, take study leave and use organizational materials for research. The sponsor may be your immediate superior within the same department. In this case the relationship may be close and supportive. The sponsor may be elsewhere in the

FIGURE 6.1 **POWER RELATIONS FOR THE ACTION RESEARCHER**
(Adapted from Greiner and Schein (1988). Reprinted with permission of Prentice-Hall Inc. Upper Saddle River, NJ)

organization, in a position of higher management. You need to work at maintaining this relationship as the continuation of the research project may depend on it. This may become particularly difficult if it emerges that the sponsor is a source of problems within the organization. You need to keep your sponsor abreast of developments and seek his or her counsel. That way you keep him or her informed and on your side.

Second, there is the sponsor's relationship to other executives. Your credibility and access may depend on the sponsor's status and standing within the organization. If the sponsor is not considered favourably by other executives, it may have a negative effect on how your research project is perceived. The sponsor's power relationship with other powers in the organization is critical in gaining acceptance for that research from higher levels of management or administration. Secondary access may be granted or denied at this level. You may have to leave the sponsor to do your access negotiation for you or you may be allowed to approach these other executives yourself. This will depend on the nature of the project. It may be that you are helpless in this regard. Whatever the project, you will have to work independently at establishing the credentials and value of the research project.

Third, there is the relationship of executives with each other. The power dynamics between departments or individual heads of departments may be a relevant feature in promoting or blocking the research. If you are from one department, that may inhibit cooperation from other departments. This may be the most significant political force for you as insider researcher, and the one over which it may be most difficult to exercise control. The key is to build personal relationships with significant persons in other departments so that they will cooperate. Perhaps some of them will be members of your project team.

The fourth relationship exists between you and significant others. Whatever the relationship between the sponsor and other executives, you must be able to establish your own relationship with significant others, many of whom may be key executives. This is particularly relevant if you wish to interview senior executives and ask what might be experienced as awkward questions. If your sponsor falls from favour, you will need to have established relationships with significant others in order to maintain your profile and project. Friedman (2001b) described the case of Marc, a middle manager, who addressed the behaviour of his CEO at a meeting of managers. At a time of closures and employees being fired, and consequent low morale and uncertainty in the organization, Marc questioned the CEO's strategy of promotions in the light of firings and low morale. The CEO subsequently sent for him privately and rebuked him strongly for questioning him in public.

The fifth relationship is between executives and others in higher management. Senior management at a corporate level may undermine the research or withdraw consent. The relationship tends to be remote, in that the executives are not likely to know you personally. It is usually unnecessary for them to have any detailed knowledge of your project. You may not have access to these people, so you may find it difficult to exercise influence over them.

The sixth relationship is between executives and organizational members. This relationship includes relationships between management and workers, and management and trade unions so that the research is accepted by the relevant parts of the organization. The research project may fall victim to ongoing organizational relationships, where employees use a lack of cooperation with you as a power tool to express dissatisfaction with some unrelated aspect of organizational life with which there is a dispute in order to gain political leverage. In these situations you are powerless and dependent on others for the resolution of the dispute.

Seventh, there are the interdepartmental relations, where some departments have more power than others, where there are different subcultures, all of which may work for or against a research project. If, for example, you work in a head office or corporate centre, you may have to deal with the attitudes of those in regional offices who view anyone from the corporate office with a prejudicious eye. The key is to establish a personal relationship with significant persons who will cooperate with you.

The eighth relationship is that of the researcher with subordinates on whom you may be relying for significant information. Subordinates may feel the need to be less than honest with their boss, who is undertaking the research. It may be that your own behaviour and management style are critical factors in the issues under investigation, and so subordinates may be reticent in providing accurate information or feedback. In such a case, where you are a superior, having a third party gather data may be essential.

The ninth relationship is that with customers or clients who may be the ultimate beneficiaries of the research or who may be involved in the actual research process. Approaching clients and customers has political complexities as it may raise expectations about the service provided to them.

Finally, there is the relationship between you and your peers. Engaging in research which involves your peers, some of whom may be friends, is particularly sensitive and may make the research process stressful. If peers and colleagues are the subject of observation and comment, they need to be informed and actively involved. They need to be protected from possible retaliation by superiors. At the same time, you need to be wary of how you can be biased in favour of peers and colleagues, be seduced by the closeness of the relationship and hence be unable to reflect and critique. Peers, colleagues and superiors may be asking the following sorts of questions: What is she observing? What is she writing about me? Am I being criticized? For those unfamiliar with an action research approach the idea of doing research in the everyday job may be hard to grasp. How can you work and include research at the same time? This question comes not only from a limited notion of what constitutes research, but also from a fear of being criticized in writing behind one's back. Pace and Argona (1991) reported how, in their internal consultancy role of champions of the quality of working life process, which involved collaborating with external consultants and unions, they lost credibility with many middle managers.

The management of the research project involves attention to all ten relationships by building support and involving key others. Ramirez and Bartunek (1989) reflected on role conflict explicitly in their case of an insider action research project in a healthcare organization. They cited two specific instances. In one instance, they noted that the insider action researcher had to deal with the twin role of facilitating meetings while at the same time acting as a department head whose status was junior relative to other participants. The second role conflict was more explicitly political. Other organizational members spread rumours about the action researcher to the effect that she was engaging in the research to set up a position for herself. The researcher's experiences of being the recipient of such political behaviours caught her off guard and were hurtful to her.

Friedman (2001b) reflects that in cases of individual research where issues are non-technical, there are likely to be insurmountable obstacles and high degrees of defensive routines. How then do you work as a 'political entrepreneur' engaging in the public performance and backstaging activities? Kakabadse (1991) presents six useful guidelines:

1   *Identify the stakeholders*: This means identifying those who have a stake or interest in the project and its outcomes and approaching them so as to identify their intentions.
2   *Work on the comfort zones*: This means working on those behaviours, values and ideas which a person can accept, tolerate or manage. As long as these are not threatened, people will be able to focus on wider concerns.
3   *Network*: This means going beyond formal hierarchies or structures where necessary to coalitions of interests which may exert greater influence on key stakeholders than the hierarchical structure.
4   *Make deals*: The making of deals is common in organizations as individuals and groups agree to support one another on a particular issue in return for support on others. This is a common way of reaching agreement on policies.

5   *Withhold and withdraw*: It may be useful on occasion to withhold information in order not to fuel opposition, though you would not want to withhold information constantly. It is also useful on occasion to withdraw from conflictual situations and let others sort out the issue.

6   *If all else fails*: Kakabadse recommends that you need to have some fall-back strategies if all else fails. These obviously depend on the demands of the situation and what you can personally handle and manage.

Friedman (2001b) provides more specific guidelines:

1   Describe your own reality image and situation as concretely as possible.
2   Ask senior and middle management if this explanation accurately fits as they see it.
3   If there are significant differences, inquire into the sources of these differences.
4   Continuously inquire into the reasoning behind actions.
5   Design strategies dealing with the current situation and similar future ones.

Lewin's force field analysis is a most useful tool to use for assessing and constructing interventions with respect to organizational political forces. As it is presented in many organization development texts, force field analysis is a technique created by Kurt Lewin for problem solving or managing change. It is based on the assumptions that in every situation there are forces driving change and forces restraining change, and that an emphasis on reducing restraining forces is more effective than increasing driving forces. While a force field might look like what we might do in listing reasons for and against taking an action, it is actually quite different. Reasons for and against are static and rational; they have to be justified. In force field analysis, forces impinging on a situation are listed. Hence, with regard to organizational politics, a force field of political driving and restraining forces may provide you with a useful insight into what is going on and help you construct interventions to reduce restraining forces. We provide a structure for using it at the end of the chapter.

Researchers often think that they have little power in the research process because they are dependent on powerful others for access. Others may see the researcher as powerful because he or she is knowledgeable, has initiated the research and is selecting whom to involve. In effect they may see the researcher's view of reality as being given public visibility. Accordingly, therefore, we need to examine some ethical issues of doing action research in your own organization.

Ethics

Ethics, in the context of research, have typically been discussed in terms of the traditional empirical research paradigms, where the focus is on researchers using subjects to obtain information to meet their own individual research objectives. Within these paradigms, ethics are taken to refer to not doing harm, not breaching confidentiality, not distorting the data, and so on.

In contrast, action research is built on participation within the system being studied. This participation is based on the assumption that the members of the system understand the process and take the significant action. Hence, ethics involves authentic relationships between the action researcher and the participants in the research – individuals, groups, organizations and communities (Rowan, 2000). Bentz and Shapiro (1998) place an emphasis on 'mindful inquiry', whereby the researcher engages in activities to prepare a space for inquiry to occur and for participants to occupy. The creation of a space is itself inquiry. Hence, the researcher looks at the possible effects of the inquiry on the participants, the self of the researcher and on the potential future of the relationship between the researcher and participants. The researcher's assumptions have an effect on all stages of the research project – topic selection, method of analysis, and so on. As Torbert (1999) puts it, action inquiry involves a certain developmental maturity in researchers to collaborate with others and expose their thought process to public testing.

Given the messiness of action research, Williamson and Prosser (2002) pose three ethical questions, which in their view, action researchers and participants need to be clear about, discuss and agree the answers:

1 If researchers and participants collaborate closely, how can confidentiality and anonymity be preserved? As action research is a political enterprise and has consequences for participants and the researchers it is difficult to guarantee anonymity and confidentiality as others can easily know who participated and may be able to identify who said or contributed what.
2 If action research is a 'journey' and 'evolves', how can informed consent be meaningful? Neither action researcher nor participants can know in advance where the journey will take them and cannot know to what they are consenting. As a change process can create its own resistance, action researchers cannot be expected to withdraw in the face of opposition (albeit by small groups within the project).

3   As action research can have political consequences how can action researchers avoid doing harm to participants? Williamson and Prosser point to two ways of answering this question: the establishment of an ethical code for action researchers, and the extent to which the collaboration and negotiation occurs so that participants own the findings as much as the researcher.

Walker and Haslett (2002) ground the issues of ethics in action research in the action research cycle itself. They suggest that ethical questions may be posed in terms of possible and actual ethical questions around the cyclical activities of planning, action and reflection. Processes of obtaining consent, ensuring anonymity and confidentiality, balancing conflicting and different needs, are actualized in planning, taking action, collecting data and interpreting. They cite Stringer's (1999) two important questions as central questions running through the whole project: Who will be affected? How will they be affected?

Clearly a significant element in both the ethics and the quality of action research is the sustainability and long-term consequences of the project. While we might not expect insider action researchers to act as 'data raiders', that is, those who drop in, collect their data and leave without regard to the long-term consequences of their actions, then you need to attend to the continuing implementation of sustaining change.

Here are some ethical issues you will need to consider and resolve:

- Negotiating access with authorities and participants.
- Promising confidentiality of information, identity and data.
- Ensuring participants the right not to participate in the research.
- Keeping relevant others informed.
- Getting permission to use documentation that was produced for other institutional purposes.
- Maintaining your own intellectual property rights.
- Keeping good faith by showing you are someone who can be trusted and always checking with others for any misunderstanding.
- Negotiating with those concerned how you will publish descriptions of their work and points of view.

Journalling is a most valuable tool for coping with and exploring political and ethical issues. As described in Chapter 3, it can be a vehicle for dumping painful experiences as well as one for articulating them and reflecting on them in a more reflective space.

Conclusions

If you are engaging in action research in your own organization, politics are powerful forces. You need to consider the impact of the process of inquiry, who the major players are, and how you can engage them in the process. Ethics involve not only not deceiving or doing harm, but being true to the process. This does not mean telling everyone everything or being politically naïve, but rather recognizing who the key political players are and how they can value the research by participating in it. It may seem that political dynamics are the major obstacle to doing action research in your own organization and it may put you off. At the same time there are those who revel in political behaviour and enjoy the cut and thrust of attempting to make a difference through their action research project.

POLITICAL ISSUES

1   Challenging the status quo: How can we do things differently?
2   Changing existing power relations: Do we have the power to change this for ourselves?
3   The system reasserting existing power relations: I don't have the authority to change this for myself.

ETHICAL DIMENSIONS

1   When I collaborate with others, how can confidentiality be maintained?
2   If my action research project is a 'journey' and 'evolves' how can informed consent be meaningful?
3   As action research can have political consequences, how can I avoid doing harm to others?

Exercise 6.1
Confronting political and ethical issues

Holian (1999) provides a case which integrates some of the themes of Chapters 5 and 6. She reports how her additional researcher role added a complex dimension to her senior executive role. She found that when organizational members provided information to her 'in confidence', there was some doubt as to whether it was in confidence to her as a researcher or as a senior executive. Merely asking informants as to which hat they saw her wearing at the time did not resolve the uncertainty. If information was provided to her as a senior executive, she may have been authorized or even obliged to act on it to prevent harm to others. If it was provided to her as a researcher, she might not have the right to do so. Whatever the role, organizational members knew she was the same person and knew what they had told her and that she could not forget it.

> **Box 6.1**
> **Ethics and**
> **role**
> **diversity in**
> **conflict**

The role conflict between her senior executive position and her action researcher role that she experienced when organizational members provided her with information which she did not know if she could use in her researcher role and which she thought she should use in her executive role, created an ethical dilemma for her.

As her research subject was ethical decision making she faced a double dilemma, a content one for her organization and a process one for the research. She established and participated in a cooperative inquiry group comprising people of decision-making roles from a diverse range of organizations. The members of this group discussed ethical issues they were experiencing, and encouraged one another to reflect on their own experience and find new ways of working with ethical issues in their own organizations.

She reported how she felt unprepared for the backlash which resulted from surfacing 'undiscussables', within the organization related to cover-ups, perceived abuse of power, nepotism, harassment, allocation of rewards and unfair discrimination. While these issues were deeper, more shocking and troubling than anticipated, she reflected that she was not adequately prepared to look after herself or others when the backlash came. Consequently, she was not able to balance the multiple roles of researcher, senior executive and programme facilitator, and after one last stand-up fight with some of her fellow senior executives, she resigned.

Force field analysis comprises five steps.

Step 1   Describe the change issue and the desired direction of the change.

Step 2   List the political forces driving change and those restraining in a diagram which has the forces in opposition to one another.

Step 3   Give a weighting to the forces, those that are stronger and more powerful than others.

Step 4   Focus on the restraining forces and assess which of the significant ones *need* to be worked on and those which *can* be worked on.

Step 5   Develop plans for reducing these forces.

Exercise 6.2
Force field analysis

7

Framing and Selecting Your Project

In this chapter we discuss how you might frame and select an action research project. When you 'frame' an issue you are naming it, and by naming it you are focusing on how you might set up its analysis and set the criteria for evaluation. Framing is a heuristic process, by which we mean that the definition of an issue already includes elements of the solution. 'Reframing' is the process whereby you question an existing frame and possibly discard it in favour of a different one (Bartunek, 1988). Then, new frames of reference need to be created to reframe the issues in such a way that problem solving can be effective.

Framing the action research project

Framing an issue can be a complex process. As we saw in the bank case in Bartunek et al. (2000), it may be that what is attractive as a research project is a practical operational issue – there is a recurring problem, which management or superiors would like researched and a solution found. In the case of the bank, the project was identified as one of improving relationships between the bank and a client. Such a research project can clearly meet criteria of being useful, particularly to management, and achievable in the research time frame and manageable for the researcher. It may also turn out as the research progresses that this apparent operational problem is more complex than it appears, requiring key people to alter their mandates and ways of thinking. We saw an example of this in the manufacturing case in Bartunek et al., where the development of an integrated manufacturing system involved radical changes in how the company did business.

The complexity of issue identification and selection illustrates that the search for an appropriate issue to study is difficult. How do you get a sense of the array of possible issues which may be addressed? By using the term 'array' we are acknowledging the existence of a wide and diverse set of issues all vying for research attention. That is not to say of course that all issues are immediately apparent to you. Some may be blatantly obvious while others may go unnoticed unless attempts are made to uncover organizational members' perceptions of key issues. Not every issue will volunteer itself automatically for resolution. It is human perception that makes the difference, thus leading us to conclude that organizational actors' interpretations are pivotal in this whole process.

While acknowledging the existence of a wide and diverse array of issues, it is important to understand that any issue once selected for attention may be embedded in a set of related issues (Beckhard and Harris, 1987). You are then confronted with choices concerning boundaries and are obliged to choose between what can be achieved within the time specified for your research and available resources.

Thinking in terms of issues, rather than problems or opportunities, which warrant attention is vital as language and labels are of the utmost importance at the outset (Dutton et al., 1983; Cooperrider and Srivastva, 1987). For example, framing proposed research initiatives in the context of addressing problems or opportunities carries some inherent risks. Framing an issue as a problem may influence who gets involved in problem resolution. It may be that organizational members embrace problems with a sense of loss, wondering about the organization's ability to reach a satisfactory resolution and often preferring to remain somewhat detached and uncommitted. The action research project may be challenging traditional procedures and ways of thinking.

Using the word 'problem' as distinct from 'opportunity' may also lead to convergent thinking (Dutton et al., 1983). The mental effort expended on problem resolution may restrict the range of alternatives considered, blinding organizational members to the possible existence of novel solutions. In a similar vein the use of the label 'opportunity' may lead to divergent thinking as this label has a greater sense of gain associated with it. Organizational members may feel a sense of excitement about tackling a significant opportunity which may have the potential for creativity.

Finally, language and labels are important as they have the potential to influence risk-taking behaviour (Dutton et al., 1983). It may be that thinking in terms of opportunities cultivates a risk-taking culture, while thinking in terms of problems cultivates a risk-averse culture. If you think with an opportunity mindset, then you are less likely to embark on a witch-hunt looking for someone to blame, as there isn't anything for which to blame them, while the mindset associated with problems embraces the notion of finding a scapegoat. It seems obvious from the above that there is merit in thinking in terms of issues without any attempt to subclassify such issues in the first instance.

What becomes important then is to uncover the issues which are viewed by organizational members as key issues warranting attention at any point in time.

In those issues which involve complex organizational change, many of these key issues may initially fall in the category of operational problem solving. As already noted, not all issues are blatantly obvious and it is therefore important for you as the researcher to get a sense of both the obvious and less obvious. It may be that the obvious is but an outward manifestation of a deeper issue which organizational members are not so willing to embrace publicly. Identification of these deeper issues may point to the need for inquiry into the fundamental assumptions which keep a problem recurring. What if the obvious only seems that way due to being ill-informed on the nature of the issue at hand? Could it be that the obvious has become so as it embraces the language of dissent and reflects the preoccupations of organizational members with consequences without ever reflecting on root causes?

As insider action researcher you need to go with the story as it evolves. As the initial questions and data demonstrate that they are inadequate for addressing the issues, you work at keeping inquiry active. You are continually testing whether consensus exists concerning the array of issues which could be addressed (Dutton and Duncan, 1987; Dutton and Jackson, 1987). Such an array may be constructed having considered organizational members' perceptions of key issues. It may embrace a healthy diversity of thinking among organizational members, or alternatively it may point to significant pockets of conflict in certain issue domains. Change triggers discussion, debate and arguments between people who champion competing ideas and proposals. Such discussion provides useful data and is desirable in order to expose different ideas to public scrutiny and examination (Buchanan and Badham, 1999).

Regardless of what the array of issues reflects, it is impossible to construct research without leaving one's own familiar world and entering into the world of others through open and honest dialogue. That of necessity means that you are willing to explore key concepts and themes and attempt to construct the perceptions of others concerning the range of issues. It involves understanding why organizational members frame such issues in the first instance, while simultaneously capturing causal relationships (Dutton et al., 1983).

We have seen that Krim's (1988) highly politicized organization did not favour or support such open inquiry. Hence, Krim's action inquiry approach was, in Torbert's (1991) view, most appropriate for insider research as it threw light on the political, organizational and personal barriers for the researcher as he worked in the social role defined within the system. We also saw how Holian's (1999) project on ethical decision making opened up what was perceived as undiscussable issues and led to conflict, resulting in Holian's resignation from the organization.

No issue in an organization is context free (Dutton and Ottensmeyer, 1987). Uncovering issues necessitates establishing not only multiple versions of 'the real facts', but also understanding the role history and experience has to play in organizational members' perceptions of these facts. In a similar manner, any given issue may be embedded in a system of political behaviour which is critical to understand if issue resolution is ever to be negotiated. Krim (1988) reported how he was told that open sharing of information in city hall was dangerous and foolhardy. Box 7.1 provides an example of how issue identification politicized a local setting.

Holley (1997) sought to inquire into how she could contribute to a living educational theory through an exploration of values in professional practice. As a head of department in a UK second-level school, she sought to explore with other teachers, by means of an appraisal system, how to enable them to reflect on their contribution to learning in the school. Independently, the management of the school introduced a classroom monitoring system, where teachers would be observed in action and assessed in terms of a checklist. This outraged Holley as she experienced this monitoring approach as a violation of her educational values. She then worked at attempting to respect, understand and listen to explorations of other teachers as they tried to make sense of their work within the prescribed monitoring system to some degree and work with a colleague in an inquiring reflective mode.

> **Box 7.1
> Issue
> identification
> and politics**

The process of identifying issues may be characterized as fluid, dynamic and emergent (Dutton et al., 1983). It is fluid in the sense that it is difficult to establish precise boundaries and when such boundaries are established they are often subject to change. It is dynamic in the sense that the core focus is subject to continuous revision as understanding deepens. It is emergent in the sense that issues appear over time. These key characteristics point to a process which is further characterized by the unfolding nature of interpretation and reinterpretation making extensive use of organizational members' judgements and revision of judgements based on insights gained from new and existing data, stimuli and perceptions.

Of immediate importance then, to you, is the need to gather and organize these data, stimuli and perceptions of yourself and others. The subsequent sense-making process points to the need for you to have good organizational and analytical capabilities. Krim (1988) kept a journal of his reflections and observations and used his academic supervisors to test them in a safe environment.

In the context of deriving meaning, it is useful at this juncture in the research process to frame issues in broad categories without attempting to attach a single dominant interpretation to any issue. The existence of multiple interpretations concerning an issue must not be eliminated. Capturing multiple and diverse interpretations adds to a deeper, richer picture of the issue at hand and holds the key to more effective resolution for the long term. In the power culture of city hall, Krim (1988) was in constant conflict regarding the interpretation of events. For example, the fact that he made notes on meetings was perceived as a tactic for manipulation.

There is an inherent danger in the process of attempting to simplify an issue by reducing ambiguity at an early stage. Such endeavours are manifested by ignoring some interpretations of an issue and attempting to attach a single dominant interpretation with a view to aiding resolution. Such a process may seem quite rational to the researcher who may be eager to get on with the task at hand. Rationality plays a role in the analysis stage but one cannot assume that rational analysis will lead to resolution. Resolution often involves a process of negotiation, embracing a sense of give and take where political interests warrant careful management. Neglecting political influences is a recipe for inaction as any proposed course of action may be planned to death and eventually be still-born.

Attaching a dominant interpretation to an issue is not necessarily bad as long as you remain cognizant of the fact that other interpretations exist and are willing to test such interpretations as the need arises. It is equally important to understand the basis for such dominance. Does the interpretation reflect a shared mind at all or almost all organizational levels, or does it reflect the shared mind of a particular group such as, for example, management or trade unions?

The extent to which a dominant interpretation of an event or issue is shared or otherwise by organizational members is important for you as the researcher, as it implies that different strategies must be employed to aid issue resolution. Where a dominant interpretation is widely shared you are more likely to gain a greater degree of commitment to the resolution process with lower levels of political activity, at least at the early stages. Where the interpretation reflects the mind of a specific group, you need to be cognizant of the fact that other groups may not share that interpretation and may choose never to share it for political reasons. Friedman (2001b) presents projects initiated by individuals on a continuum, with technical issues at one extreme and non-technical at the other. In his view technical operational issues are easier to have support for, while non-technical issues are harder to influence and are embedded in organizational defensive routines. Krim (1988) reported that the most powerful union leader did not support the labour–management cooperation programme, while other government personnel did. Box 7.2 provides an example of managing politics as the issues were framed.

Quinlan (1996), a clinical psychologist in a mental health unit, sought to inquire into his own professional practice as well as how roles played in multidisciplinary teams and the wider organization interacted and shaped professional practice. He sought to collaborate with his colleagues to inquire into 'complex cases', as instanced in the case of an individual client so as to develop mutual collaboration. This cooperative inquiry venture into good practice, which he referred to as 'working with downstairs', had only partial success. After some time, his peer group unilaterally decided to hold meetings with other professionals, rather than continue with the client-focused case meetings that he had initiated. At the same time, he was working with senior management, which he calls 'working with upstairs'. In this group the focus was on power and interaction was marked by confrontation. Accordingly, his desire to remain in the organization was both an enabling and restraining force on the way he constructed and dealt with power dynamics.

Box 7.2 Project framing and organizational politics

Finally, it is important when categorizing issues that each issue is framed in the context of its implicit and explicit assumptions, any known causal relationships, and any predictive judgements concerning the speed of issue resolution (Dutton et al., 1983). Making assumptions explicit aids the resolution process as organizational members develop a shared understanding of the issue being addressed in terms of its history, scope and possible outcomes. Establishing causal relationships helps to place an issue in context by grounding it in organizational reality while simultaneously establishing how organizational members attribute certain outcomes to root causes. Outlining predictive judgements attaches a sense of urgency or otherwise to the issue at hand.

Selecting the research project

Having identified a range of issues, you are confronted with selecting an issue or issues for immediate attention in the context of a specific research agenda. Before making a final selection you are well advised to reflect on each issue identified from personal and organizational perspectives with a view to establishing:

- the degree to which it offers an opportunity to experiment with existing and/or newly acquired knowledge;
- the degree to which it offers opportunities for personal growth and learning;
- the degree to which issue resolution offers the possibility of increasing your profile within the organization;
- the balance between personal gain and organizational gain in the event of successful resolution;
- the degree to which the issue may be resolved within known resource and time constraints.

Conclusions

Framing and selecting an action research project is a complex project. What appears clear at the outset may lose its apparent clarity as the project unfolds. How you frame and subsequently reframe the project may hold important learning for you. The critical issue for you is to be able to frame and select a project from a position of being close to the issue. The acts of framing and selecting your action research project are themselves action research learning cycles. In other words, you do your initial framing, reflect on how that framing fits or not, articulate some understanding of why that framing fits or does not fit and then take action accordingly and so test that situation. Similarly, you make your initial selection, test it and adapt according to the data generated by the selection and framing processes.

As I look at my organization/section in which I work:

1   What questions arise out of my experience to which I would like to search for answers?
2   What might be the answers to these questions?
3   What do I think might be the underlying causes of the situation for which I have these questions?
4   What alternative answers might exist?
5   Where do I fit into the situation as defined by the question?
6   What would other members of the organization think of me working on this issue?
7   What opposition will I encounter?
8   Where are the sensitive issues?
9   What are the constraints?
10   Who needs to be involved? Whose support do I enlist?
11   Where would be a good place to begin?
12   How will I engage in uncovering the data?

Part III
Implementation

8

Implementing Your Action
Research Project

In this chapter we explore how you may implement an action research project in a system, whether in an organization, be it a company, a hospital, a school or a unit/department or service within your organization. In Chapter 3, we outlined the skills you require. The action research process in your own organization follows the action research cycle introduced in Chapter 2. This involves:

1 Systematically generating and collecting research data about an ongoing system relative to some objective or need.
2 Feeding the data back to relevant others.
3 Conducting a collaborative analysis of the data.
4 Planning and taking collaborative action based on the diagnosis.
5 Jointly evaluating the results of that action, leading to further planning.

So the cycle is repeated.

The process of change

How do you go about implementing the action research cycle in a planned way in a large system? While actor-directors go with the story in their film-making, they also create and follow a script. The process whereby the action research agenda is identified and worked through has been well articulated by Richard Beckhard (Beckhard and Harris, 1987; Beckhard and Pritchard, 1992). Beckhard's framework has four phases:

1 Determining the need for change.
2 Defining the future state.

3   Assessing the present in terms of the future to determine the work to be done.
4   Managing the transition.

As we discussed in Chapter 6, doing action research in your own organization is intensely political and involves you in concurrent and sometimes conflicting roles. We think that it is important to remind you that managing the political system at every step is more important than any rigid adherence to an idealized picture of how these steps might work.

Determining the need for change

The preferred starting place is to inquire into the context for change in the organization, unit or subunit. It may seem obvious that naming the need for change and its causes is essential. The forces for change may be coming from the external environment, such as global market demands, developing customer needs, and so on. They may be coming from the internal environment, such as budget over-runs, low morale among staff, excessive dysfunctional political intergroup rivalry, and so on. The diagnosis of these forces identifies their source, their potency and the nature of the demands they are making on the system. These forces for change have to be assessed so that major change forces are distinguished from the minor ones.

A second key element in evaluating the need for change is the degree of choice about whether to change or not. This is often an overlooked question. Choices are not absolute. While there may be no control over the forces demanding change, there is likely to be a great deal of control over how to respond to those forces. In that case there is likely to be a good deal of scope as to what changes, how, and in what time-scale the change can take place. The action research cycle enables shared diagnosis into how these forces for change are having an impact and what choices exist to confront them. The outcome of determining the need for change is to ask a further question, which is whether first- or second-order change is required. By first-order change is meant an improvement in what the organization does or how it does it. By second- or third-order change is meant a system-wide change in the nature of the core assumptions and ways of thinking and acting. The choice of whether to follow a first- or second-order change process may be as much determined by organizational politics as by the issues under consideration. How the key organizational actors interpret the forces for change and how they form their subsequent judgement as to what choices they have are important political dynamics.

Defining the desired future

Once a sense of the need for change has been established, the most useful focus for attention is to define a desired future state. This process is essentially that of articulating what the organization, unit or subunit would look like after change has taken place. This process is critical as it helps provide focus and energy because it describes the desires for the future in a positive light. On the other hand, an initial focus on the problematic or imperfect present may over-emphasize negative experiences and generate pessimism. Working at building consensus on a desired future is an important way of harnessing the political elements of the system.

Assessing the present in terms of the future to determine the work to be done

When the desired future state is articulated, you then attend to the present reality and ask, 'What is it in the present which needs changing in order to move to the desired future state?' Because the present is being assessed in the light of the desired future, it is assessing what needs changing and what does not. It may judge that, for the change to take place effectively, a change in current structures, attitudes, roles, policies or activities may be needed. As any change problem is a cluster of possible changes, it may need to group particular problems under common headings, such as, HRM policies and practices, service delivery, information management, reward systems, organizational structure and design, and so on. Then it describes the problem more specifically and asks, 'Which of these requires priority attention? If A is changed, will a solution to B fall easily into place? What needs to be done first?' This step is about taking a clear, comprehensive, accurate view of the current state of the organization, involving an organizational diagnosis which names:

- the priorities within the constellation of change problems;
- the relevant subsystems where change is required;
- an assessment of the readiness and capability for the contemplated change.

Another element in describing the present is to describe the relevant parts of the organization that will be involved in the change. This description points to the critical people needed for the change to take place. This is an explicit consideration of the political system and where you draw on your skills as a 'political entrepreneur'. Examples of who needs to be involved might include specific managers, informal leaders, IT specialists and so on. Their readiness and capability for change must be assessed. *Readiness* points to the motivation and willingness to change, while *capability* refers to whether they are able, psychologically and otherwise, to change.

Implementing the change and managing the transition

This step is what is generally perceived as being the actual change process though, as we have seen, preparation for change is equally essential. The critical task is to move from the present to the future and manage the intervening period of transition. This transition state between the present and the future is typically a difficult time because the past is found to be defective and no longer tenable and the new state has not yet come into being. So, in essence, the transition state is somewhat particular, as the old has gone and the new has not yet been realized, and so needs to be seen and managed as such.

There are two aspects to managing this transition state. One is having a strategic and operational plan which simply defines the goals, activities, structures, projects and experiments that will help achieve the desired state. As no amount of change can take place without commitment, the second aspect is a commitment plan. The commitment plan focuses on who in the organization must be committed to the change if it is to take place. There may be particular individuals whose support is a prerequisite for the change and a critical mass whose commitment is necessary to provide the energy and support for the change to occur. The political dynamics of building commitment involves finding areas of agreement and compromise among conflicting views and negotiating cooperation (Fisher and Ury, 1986; Ury, 1991).

It is at the management of transition stage that you are likely to make most use of a group which works with you as the core project team. While you are the one doing the dissertation, this group is an organizational project group which contains both technical competence and hierarchical status to manage the project. Hence there is a need for you to be able to build and maintain the team (Wheelan, 1999).

Beckhard's (1997) change process developed out of his action research approach and it involves continuous interaction between diagnosis, planning, action and review in order to move a change through a system (see Figure 8.1). Action research has a large degree of messiness and unpredictability about it, in that it is research on real-life action. As the story unfolds unforeseen events are likely to occur. Environmental events may create a crisis in the organization; fellow key actors may change and so on. The action researcher as actor-director is both creating and acting a script.

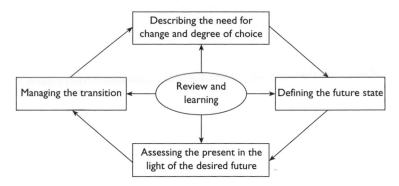

FIGURE 8.1 **THE PROCESS OF CHANGE**

Review and learning

The critical dimension to action research is how review is undertaken and managed. Review is essentially reflection on experience and in any such reflection the critical questions are asked, not to evoke guilt or blame, but to generate learning as to what is taking place and what needs to be adjusted. If review is undertaken in this spirit then the likelihood of individual or team defensiveness can be lessened and learning can take place. As we explored in Chapter 2, learning comes out of reviewing the process and examining emergent questions about content, process and premise. Box 8.2 at the end of the chapter provides an example of the use of Beckhard and Harris's framework.

Learning by design

An alternative approach to the Beckhard change process framework and those developed from it is the 'learning by design' approach (Shani and Docherty, 2003). Learning by design is an approach which builds alternative design configurations through implementing specific learning mechanisms, using action research and other collaborative approaches. Its basic premise is that organizations that prioritize the development and full utilization of their personnel and aim to achieve optimal economic results must explore alternative designs to the bureaucratic organization. These alternatives come about through sustainable learning. Shani and Docherty present six extensive case examples of this approach, across different industries and from them outline a generic eight phase process:

- *Phase 1*: Project initiation – initial definition of purpose and scope, initial system scanning, securing managerial commitment and role, align intervention with business strategy, establish criteria and measurement of success, review alternative mechanisms to lead effort.
- *Phase 2*: Formation of mechanisms to lead the learning by design efforts.
- *Phase 3*: Developing a shared vision.
- *Phase 4*: Systematic inquiry, analysis and reflection on currently used learning mechanisms.
- *Phase 5*: Identification and exploration (of fit) of alternative/additional learning mechanisms.
- *Phase 6*: Developing the design of a 'blueprint' for action.
- *Phase 7*: Implementation of changes – improvement processes for existing learning mechanisms and implementation of new learning mechanisms.
- *Phase 8*: Reflection on the 'learning by design' planned change process.

In our view, the learning by design approach can be integrated with insider action research through the process champions or leaders attending to the dynamics that they engage in and how they draw on their preunderstanding, reflect on role duality and manage organizational politics in their efforts to develop learning mechanisms in their own organizational systems.

We cautioned earlier against limiting action research to being a logical and clinical process, where individuals and groups move through the action research steps in a rational, albeit politically aware, manner. However, such approaches are not exclusive. It is not uncommon for researchers to utilize story-telling, drama or photography as a core process of their data generation (Marshall, 1995). Evans (1997) studied her own practice as a deputy head of a large second level school in the UK. Within a hierarchically organized institution she worked with teachers collaboratively, enabling the creation of a learning community through dialogue in which they took ownership of their own development, established value positions and supported one another. She created case studies out of her experiences in the school, and presented them as stories to the group. For example, she composed one story, titled, 'Just Tell Me What to Do' out of her own experience. The other teachers were able to relate to the story as it reflected school culture. This and other stories enabled the teachers to reframe their perspectives and to explore new perspectives together.

Data generation as intervention

In action research data comes through engagement with others in the action research cycles. Therefore, it is important to know that acts which are intended to collect data are themselves interventions. So asking an individual a question or observing him or her at work is not simply collecting data but is also *generating* learning data for both you, the researcher, and the individual concerned. In short, you are not neutral. Every action, even the very intention and presence of research, is an intervention and has political implications across the system. Accordingly, it is more appropriate to speak of data *generation* than data gathering.

For you as the insider action researcher, data generation comes through active involvement in the day-to-day organizational processes relating to the action research project. As the researcher in your own organization, you are an inconspicuous observer, as your presence is taken for granted. Your observations are made as a member of the organization in the day-to-day interactions with colleagues and others. Not only are data generated through participation in and observation of teams at work, problems being solved, decisions being made and so on, but also through the interventions which are made to advance the project. Some of these observations and interventions are made in formal settings – meetings and interviews; many are made in informal settings – over coffee, lunch and other recreational settings.

You will need to document your reflections for all these occasions. Apart from your journalling activities which typically take place in private, there are the situations at meetings where you want to take notes or jot down reflections. This, of course, is a sensitive process as appearing to take notes may create suspicion. A useful rule of thumb is to adopt what others are doing. If at a meeting most people take notes, then it is acceptable for you to take notes. If no one is taking notes, then you do not take notes. In that case, you try to jot down your reflections afterwards, as soon as possible, while events are fresh in your memory.

When you observe the dynamics of groups at work – for example, communication patterns, leadership behaviour, use of power, group roles, norms, elements of culture, problem solving and decision making, relations with other groups – you are provided with the basis for inquiry into the underlying assumptions and their effects on the work and life of these groups (Schein, 1999a, 1999b). As you are dealing with directly observable phenomena in the organizations with which you are working, the critical issue for you is how to inquire into what you are observing and, at the same time, be helpful to the system. For example, at a team meeting you may notice all sorts of behaviour which you suspect affects how the team goes about its work – people not listening to each other, wandering off the agenda and so on. If you make an intervention into these areas you are aiming to focus on what is useful for the advancement of the action research project, rather than what you have observed. Without this discipline you may reflect what you have observed, but the observation may not be owned by participants in the system because it does not meet their needs as experienced or it appears to be showing how clever you are in observing these things. For you, observation and inquiry into how the systemic relationship between the individual, the team, the interdepartmental group and the organization operates is critical to the complex nature of organizational problem solving and issue resolution (Rashford and Coghlan, 1994).

You may consider using some form of survey instrument (Nadler, 1977). An action research approach suggests that data-gathering tools need to be designed to fit both the organizational setting and the purpose of the research (Coghlan and McAuliffe, 2003). While surveying employees by questionnaire as to their views on some aspects of their work or the organization tends to be seen merely as a method of collecting information, it is more important to see how it is an intervention. The reception of a questionnaire by employees may generate questioning, suspicion, anxiety, enthusiasm – all of which are real data for you. If you ignore this you may be missing a key element of how the organizational problem exists and does not get solved and indeed what issues lie ahead in the research process.

In a similar vein, interviewing in action research is not simply a tool for collecting data. As we have pointed out, asking someone a question or a series of questions is a data-generating intervention. Interviewing in action research tends to be open-ended and unstructured, focusing on what the interviewee has to say, rather than confirming any hypothesis the action researcher might have. In Chapter 3, we presented a typology of interview techniques, pure inquiry, exploratory-diagnostic inquiry and confrontive inquiry (Schein, 1999a). As we emphasized in that chapter, combining inquiry with advocacy is a critical skill for the insider action researcher.

While a distinction is made between the study of formal documentation (what Gummesson calls 'desk research') and interviews, Gummesson (2000) makes the point that these are artificial distinctions as the researcher is faced with a continuous flow of data. Secondary data are data both numeric and textual that were developed for some purpose other than helping to solve the action research question in hand. You need to evaluate these data on the basis of their relevance to the research question, their availability and accuracy. In order to have confidence in the worth, validity and reliability of the data, you need to consider the following questions for each archival source:

1   Who collected the data?
2   When was it collected?
3   What was collected?
4   Why was it collected?

Studying relevant documentation can be an important part of organizational research. Access to documentation is integrally linked to the level of access to engage in research. Reports, memos, minutes of meetings and so on may be highly confidential and access to them may depend on the degree to which an organization's management is willing to grant access to the inside researcher. Other documentation may be held in archives in the organization or in libraries. Hill (1993) provides both a general introduction and practical guide to using archives. Box 8.1 provides an example of the use of archival documentation.

One of the central issues for Coghlan (1996) at the outset of his research was to discover what relevant documentation existed and how it could be found. As he had been a member of the organization's central administration team on two occasions he had both a general sense of the chronology and significance of events and a good deal of prior information as to what had happened, when and what documentation was extant. Documentation reviewed fell into three groupings:

**Box 8.1
Using
archives**

1   Documentation circulated to the organization and accessible to all members, such as letters from the executives, texts of executive addresses given on special occasions, policy statements, and reports of some task forces.
2   Documentation internal to the central administration: staff memos, minutes of staff meetings, reports of consultations, terms of reference for task forces and consultations, and summaries of policy developments for internal use.
3   Confidential documentation.

An important element of Coghlan's preunderstanding as a former member of the central administration team, was his inside knowledge of

cont.

both the content of the research and the system in the archives. In one instance it was by leafing through an unmarked folder that key material was uncovered accidentally; he knew the material existed but could not find it in catalogued files. There were many instances of undated documents, the dates of which could only be pieced together by inside knowledge of when these issues were under consideration. There were instances of where the author knew from his experience that certain files/documents existed, but could not find them in the archives. On many occasions these were found in other parts of the office complex.

Coghlan worked from his experience and prior knowledge of the history of policy development in the organization. In asking what was in the archives, he knew that minutes of meetings, drafts of policy, letters and addresses, many reports and so on, existed. He had used them himself in his work as a staff member and internal consultant. The issue of how comprehensive and systematic the documentation would be in facilitating a large-scale research project was unknown. In general the documentation was more than adequate in providing the information required to put data together for the purposes required by his research.

Coghlan's position as a member of the organization and an internal consultant was significant in the data gathering. He had unrestricted access to the archives. He had extensive knowledge of the period and experience of the issues under research and his familiarity with the administration offices facilitated the uncovering and evaluation of relevant material.

What were the criteria by which the documentation was judged to be relevant? As the purpose of studying the documentation was to uncover primary sources, the criteria were that the documents studied showed what intentions were articulated, what was done, what was said about what was done and so on.

The role of technology in the change process

Technology has transformed the world of communication. Within organizations, communication through e-mail, websites and intranets have become the norm. Virtual team meetings transcend boundaries of time and space. Information technology (IT) is increasingly becoming the standard method for communication between people and organizations. Technology is also shaping the development of organizational processes in relation to human resource development (Church et al., 2001) and organizational change (Coghlan and McDonagh, 2001). Indeed, as Coghlan and McDonagh point out, some of the major dilemmas confronting organizational change are specifically related to the introduction and integration of information technology into organizations and which, in their view, action research can make a major contribution to their resolution.

The roles information technology can play in your action research process are manifold. You can use technology to gather information, process it and present conclusions. You can use technology to communicate with your co-researchers, colleagues and clients, on a one-to-one basis, to hold virtual group meetings and to communicate with large numbers of people. In regard to this latter use of information technology, an important challenge for you, as the action researcher, is to attend to the quality of participation that occurs through the technology. As Schein (2003) points out, the absence of 'functional familiarity', that is the experience we build up of working with individuals in a face-to-face manner where we know how to read their responses, their body language and general way of interacting, can become a severe limitation on collaborative processes.

How do you know when to stop?

Action research projects which act as dissertations typically have an inbuilt time schedule. Especially within single-year or two-year masters programmes, you are expected to do your action research project within a designated time period in order that you may meet the requirements of the programme to which you are attached. Accordingly, you may take your submission deadline, the amount of time you are going to give yourself for writing the dissertation and work back to where your organizational story will end. In many respects, the decision you make as to when your story will end is arbitrary. At the same time it is important to set a date, after which, whatever takes place, however exciting and relevant, will not be included in your story.

When completion deadlines have more flexibility, your decision to stop is still arbitrary and may depend on your judgement as to the extent that your project has yielded sufficient learning.

Conclusions

In this chapter we have explored how you might go about implementing an action research project. We have shown that, after determining the need for it, it is useful to work at articulating a desired future before getting into details of what to do and how to build commitment to the action. Accordingly, you need to keep in mind that everything you do is an intervention and that you need to be sensitive to the impact that asking questions and observing have on participants. You need to manage the politics of the situation at all times.

Deane (2004) was the chief executive of an ad hoc government agency Oldorg, whose role was to set, monitor and certify standards for vocational education and training programmes provided within the public further education sector. Under new government legislation, 'Oldorg' was replaced by a new agency, 'Neworg', established in 2001, which subsumed the existing functions of Oldorg and considerably extended its remit. Deane undertook an action learning project to explore how learning could support change in an organization. It involved designing and implementing a learning programme for staff of Oldorg at a time of great uncertainty for the organization, and in a context of vigorous internal and external debate surrounding the introduction of the new legislation.

Deane reports how she adopted Beckhard and Harris's (1987) framework for implementing in Oldorg. A vision of the future had been formulated, by examining the given and the possible dimensions of the change arising from the legislation. There had also been an analysis of the present state and an identification of key change issues, focusing in particular on the cultural aspects. What was needed was to complete the process by managing the transition to the changed state. This called for a high level of openness to change across the whole organization. In effect, it called for a dynamic and continuous learning process at both individual and organizational level, to cope with the rate of change in the external environment. While in the past Oldorg had worked through change by learning in a largely intuitive and informal way, Deane now proposed to adopt a more systematic approach. This would closely link

Box 8.2 Implementing change in your own organization

cont.

the themes of learning and change, first to effect change through learning, and second to discover how change could act as a catalyst for learning.

Deane recognized that it was her responsibility to prepare the organization for the future, to predict and plan for change, to influence the change process, and to protect and preserve what was important to the organization in the new situation. She was aware that this presented a great challenge to her leadership: a great deal depended on managing the process effectively, both within and outside the organization.

Having identified the major reasons *why* change was necessary, she moved towards answering the second question: *What* needs to change? She saw how the new organizations would have to develop new relationships with stakeholders, serve new customers, adopt new processes and new technologies, and provide new products and services to a bigger market. She reports that she found the notion of a 'constellation' of change issues with a complex set of interrelationships between them particularly helpful. Allied to the notion that it is almost impossible to change only one thing, this concept helped her to frame a change agenda for Oldorg. Focusing mainly on the cultural aspects of change, for which it was suggested by the earlier analysis that the organization's readiness was low, the action learning project then sought an answer to the final question: *How* can we change?

Drawing on her reading on organizational learning and the learning organization, a learning programme was designed and implemented. Simply stated, the purpose of the programme was to ensure that all staff members were given the opportunity to participate in focused learning activities to help them prepare for the changes ahead. The programme combined a number of learning modes, targeted at producing specific learning outcomes for individuals and for the organization as a whole. Political, technical and culture change issues were explored by means of a learning audit, project teams, action learning groups, staff seminars, future focus group and training. In terms of culture, the openness of communication and information sharing enabled a high level of ownership of the change. In technical terms, participation in training and new skill development led to new technology systems to prepare for the post-legislation organization. In political terms, the future focus group's

cont.

submission was accepted and contributed to the development of the process.

Deane reflects on the whole action learning process in first-, second- and third-person terms. For herself applying the principles of general management to herself and the public sector and being challenged by the action learning setting was the important learning for her. In second-person terms, the organization learned to change and was well adapted to meet the challenges of the new organization. In third-person terms, there was a major impact for the clients of the new organization in that they would be able to gain credits for action research undertaken in a work context or elsewhere. The new organization would have a flexible assessment approach to meet the needs of learners.

Exercise 8.1
The process of
implementation
	Step 1 Determining the need for change:
	    ● What are the external forces driving change?
	    ● What are the internal forces driving change?
	    ● How powerful are these forces?
	    ● What choices do we have?
	Step 2 If things keep going the way they are without significant intervention:
	    ● What will be the predicted outcome?
	    ● What is our alternative desired outcome?
	Step 3 What is it in the present that we need to change in order to get to our desired future – what is done, how work is done, structures, attitudes, culture?
	Step 4
	    ● What are the main avenues which will get us from here to there?
	    ● What are the particular projects within those avenues – long, medium, short term?
	    ● How do we involve the organization in this project?
	    ● Where do we begin?
	    ● What actions do we take to create maximum effect, medium effect, minimum effect?
	
	                                                          cont.

- How will we manage the transition?
- How do we build commitment? Who is/is not ready/capable for change? How will we manage resistance?
- Who will let it happen, help it happen, make it happen?
- Do we need additional help – consultants, facilitators?

Step 5

- What review procedures do we need to establish?
- How do we articulate and share what we are learning?

9

Interlevel Dynamics in Action Research

Levels of analysis are commonly used as frameworks for researching, understanding and intervening in organizational systems (Harrison and Shirom, 1999). Levels of analysis typically refer to the identification of issues at units of complexity, such as the individual, the group, intergroup and the organization. They are important dimensions of action research as traditionally they are seen as targets for action research. This chapter extends the traditional focus of levels of analysis as the target for action research to the notion of levels of aggregation or interlevel dynamics and how interlevel dynamics are important in doing action research in your own organization (Coghlan, 2002). Interlevel dynamics illuminate first-, second- and third-person practice.

Levels of complexity – individual, group, intergroup, organizational – are frequently used as frameworks for understanding organizational processes. Several essential points need to be made about the concept and usage of the term levels. First, the notion of levels must be distinguished from that of echelon (Rousseau, 1985). Echelon refers to a position on a chain of command in an organization, such as worker, supervisor, manager, group manager and chief executive. The less common use of organizational levels as a construct in organizational behaviour, however, describes levels of complexity.

Rashford and Coghlan (1994) present levels in terms of how people participate in organizations and link them to provide a useful tool for the manager, consultant and teacher of organizational behaviour. They distinguish four levels of behaviour in organizations: the individual, the face-to-face team, the interdepartmental group and the organizational. The first level is the *bonding* relationship that the individual has with the organization and the organization with the individual. For the individual, this involves a utilization of membership and participation in the organization in order to meet personal life goals, while for management the core issue is to get a person committed to the goals, values and culture of the organization. The more complex approach to participation exists in establishing *effective working relationships in a face-to-face team*. An even more complex involvement exists in terms of the interdepartmental group type of interface where teams must be *coordinated* in order to achieve complex tasks and maintain a balance of power among competing political interest groups. Finally, the most complex, from the point of view of the individual, is the relationship of the total organization to its external environment in which other organizations are individual competitors, competing for scarce resources to produce similar products or services. The key task for any organization is its ability to *adapt* to environmental forces driving for change.

When you are working at each or any of the levels described above, you will typically find that you are challenged to include the other levels in your diagnosis and intervention. For instance, you may be working with a team on an aspect of your action research project. In the process of this work, it emerges that some of the individual members are experiencing dissatisfaction with their relationship with the organization and do not provide optimal contributions to the team's endeavours. Or it may be that the flow of information from other teams is having a negative effect on the work of the team with which you are working. In these instances, you are challenged to move beyond the team level intervention in which you are engaged to consider dynamics at the other levels, which are having an impact on the team.

Organizational levels are important dynamics in organizational politics. Organizational political behaviour may be individual, team and interdepartmental group. Individuals may engage in covert political behaviour in order to advance their own standing in the organization. Teams may engage in overt or covert political behaviour to gain advantage over others in order to obtain more resources.

Levels of analysis in action research

Action research at the individual level

In Chapter 3 we explored how you can engage in first-person practice by attending to your own learning-in-action. In Chapter 4 we located situations where the primary intended focus of the research is first-person in Quadrant 3. First-person research in your own organization, that is how the research is for you, is linked to your own sense of bonding to your organization. As we have seen, how the research contributes to your own development, your role and future in the organization is a significant aspect of undertaking research in your own organization. Accordingly, your own self-awareness, closeness to the issues, how you frame the issues and so on are critical first-person processes of which you have to be aware and to work on consciously as part of the action research project. Your own individual learning and level change as you attend to your own learning-in-action through your first-person action research projects. Individual learning-in-action typically involves being able to reflect on experience, understand it and enact chosen alternative behaviours and learn to critique your assumptions in a manner which exposes your private inferences to public testing. The degree to which the project enhances your career or to which it decreases your motivation to remain in the organization is important. We saw how an outcome of Holian's engagement in her project resulted in her resignation from her organization. So a central element of the individual level for the insider action researcher is the management of role duality, politics and ethics as we explored in Chapters 5 and 6.

Action research at the group or team level

Second-person research is characterized when researchers engage with others in conversation and action. This may be actualized in one-to-one situations where you engage in action and reflection with a single individual. More frequently second-person practice is enacted in groups, whether in the formal organizational hierarchical teams or the temporary committees or task forces that are built around the project. They may be collegial groups which you have set up to explore the task of your action research project, such as a cooperative inquiry or action learning group.

The experience of groups and teams in engaging in the action research steps is paramount. As they engage in the activities of diagnosing, planning and taking action they may experience some success in some of their activities and not in others. They may experience internal conflict and destructive political behaviour by some members. They may struggle to reach agreement on strategies and action and so on. What is important is that groups and teams learn to reflect on their experience in terms of how they function as groups and teams. This involves attending to task issues of how they do the task and relational issues of how they manage communication among themselves, solve problems, make decisions, manage conflict and so on (Schein, 1999a). Exploring these issues means being able to go beyond personal blame and draw on useful constructs on effective group and team development to take remedial action where necessary and develop effective team processes (Wheelan, 1999). These activities involve content, process and premise issues as the issues on which they are working are studied and the ways in which the teams work are reviewed and underlying assumptions uncovered and examined. Bartunek (2003) provides an illustration of the development on change agent teams over time in terms of identity, actions and stakeholder relationships. She narrates cognitive and affective links between: how identity evolved over time in the face of member turnover, explicit reminders of identity and face-to-face contact; how actions intended were taken and how emotionally engaging the actions were; and how efforts to make these stakeholder relationships positive were taken.

Action research at the intergroup level

Yet the research and change process cannot be restricted to learning and change by individuals and teams alone. A further application of second-person research is how the learning and change which takes place in individuals and teams needs to be generalized across the interdepartmental group, whereby other teams and units engage in dialogue and negotiation. A critical focus for attention in this regard is the impact on the change process of cultural perspectives from the viewpoint of different functions (Schein, 1992). Intergroup dialogue needs to take account of how functional areas in organizations hold different assumptions from and about one another.

Groups and teams do not work in isolation. They are typically members of wider systems and such membership involves intergroup dynamics, such as being interdependent in a work flow or information process. The consequences of intergroup interdependence are intergroup dynamics, such as the sharing of information, negotiation over resources, intergroup prejudice and intergroup conflict. You can expect to have intergroup dynamics in any project involving a complex system. Indeed, working at the intergroup level is an extension of second-person research. The interdepartmental group experiences the differences between groups, as different groups are separated from one another by what they do, by location and by their interests. Accordingly, any action research work which involves members of separate departments working together must take account of how each department has its own concerns, its own view of the world, its own political interests in the work of the project and may even have its own terminology and language. We would argue that interdepartmental group work is essentially intercultural (Schein, 1992).

A further instance of action research at the intergroup level is found in the burgeoning use of large-group interventions in organizational change. Large-group interventions are described as search conferences, future search, dialogue conferences open space, real time strategic change, among others (Gustavsen and Englestad, 1986; Holman and Devane, 1999; Martin, 2001), and are gatherings of the members of a system in a large group in order to create common ground for the future development of that system.

Action research at the organizational level

Finally, the action research project does not stop within the organization. Organizations as open systems have a dynamic two-way relationship with their external environments (Katz and Kahn, 1978). The second-person research process includes how the organization is affecting and being affected by, its customers or clients, stakeholders, local community, competitors, wider society and other organizations. Action research at the organizational level means that the project encompasses the organization as an entity in a competitive economic and social environment. The project therefore is inclusive of the organization's relationship with its external stakeholders such as customers, clients and competitors, as well as in internal stakeholders at the individual, groups and intergroup levels.

To add further complexity, the project may involve inter-organizational work, typically called inter-organizational networking. Inter-organizational networking is where member organizations deliberately develop voluntary networks to help deal with complex issues and devise collaborative ways of planning and taking action. As Chisholm (1998, 2001) describes, action research is essential for engaging in network development and contributes to planning, action and learning processes. The learning steps of the action research cycle need to be inclusive of reflection on how different mindsets and political interests are experiencing working together, how they process and interpret that experience and take action accordingly.

Interlevel dynamics in action research

Viewing organizations through levels of analysis is only one part of the picture. The other part refers to how levels are related to each other. In an organization, there is an essential interlevel element in that each level (the individual, the group/team, the interdepartmental group, the organization) has a dynamic relationship with each of the others (Rashford and Coghlan, 1994). This relationship is grounded in systems dynamics, whereby the relationship each level has with each of the others is systemic, with feedback loops forming a complex pattern of relationships (McCaughan and Palmer, 1994; Haslebo and Nielsen, 2000). For instance, dysfunctions at any level can lead to dysfunctions at any of the others. An individual's level of disaffection may be expressed in dysfunctional behaviour in the team and affect a team's ability to function effectively, which in turn reinforces the individual's disaffection. If a team is not functioning effectively, it can limit the interdepartmental group's effectiveness, which may depend on the quality and timeliness of information, resources and partially completed work from that team. If the interdepartmental group's multiple activities are not coordinated, the organization's ability to compete effectively may be affected. In systemic terms, each level affects each of the others. Viewing organizational levels as simply 'levels of analysis', without taking interlevel dynamics into consideration, misses the point about the systemic relationship the individual has with the team, the team with the individual, the team with other teams, the organization with its environment and each with each other.

Action research involves work with individuals, teams, across the interdepartmental group, organization and between organizations. It also involves work between these levels as an individual has an effect on the team and vice versa, teams affect other teams and an organization's effectiveness is partly dependent on how individuals, teams and the interdepartmental group are in alignment (Rashford and Coghlan, 1994) (see Figure 9.1).

Many of the case examples cited through the book, while appearing to focus on one unit of analysis, actually contain interlevel dynamics. Krim

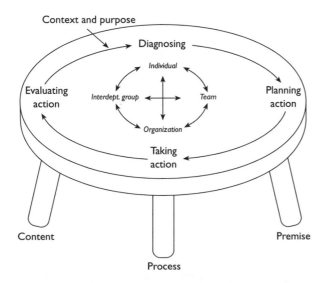

FIGURE 9.1 **ORGANIZATIONAL DYNAMICS OF ACTION RESEARCH**

(1988), while focusing on learning was embroiled in complex interlevel dynamics in his engagement with key political players and groups in city hall. In OilCo, the CEO formed his managers into an executive council (Kleiner and Roth, 2000). The managers had not worked together as a team before, so it was a new experience for them to do so. They formed subteams to work on particular projects. The executive council disseminated its work to the wider organization through a learning convention, at which people spoke frankly for the first time about their views of the company and dialogue began to take place. The process continued through the company, whereby the transformation of fundamental ways of thinking and feeling moved from the CEO to the executive council and through the organization and impacted teams and individuals.

Conclusions

Levels of analysis are commonly used as frameworks for researching, understanding and intervening in organizational systems. Levels of analysis typically refer to the identification of issues at units of complexity, such as the individual, the group, the intergroup and organization. They are an important dimension of action research as traditionally they are seen as targets for action research. This chapter reviewed the traditional focus of levels of analysis as targets for action research and extends the notion to levels of aggregation or interlevel dynamics.

Interlevel dynamics are also operative for you as an action researcher in the action research process itself. You engage in interlevel dynamics as you encounter the process of the complex systems in which you enact action research projects. Your engagement in first- and second-person research typically requires enactment of your own learning-in-action along with work with groups, between groups and with organizations in their environments. The application of interlevel dynamics to first and second person is an important dimension of both understanding and enacting the experiential cycles of action research.

You may use the construct of the four levels as a diagnostic framework by being aware of the issues occurring at each level and how one level affects another, and be able to work with individuals, teams and interteam groups to evaluate the effect of one level on another. For instance, the process of moving a change through an organization requires a systemic view of the complex interrelationship and interdependence of the individual, the face-to-face team, the interdepartmental group and the organization.

Interlevel dynamics are systemic processes. They provide frames for us to understand how participation in human systems is developed through increasing complexity as individuals, individuals in groups and teams, individuals in groups and teams which are part of an interdepartmental group with other groups and teams, the interdepartmental group within an organization which itself is a participant in a sector, a market and global economy. These frames are not only for the purpose of understanding but are also the basis for action (Rashford and Coghlan, 1994). As Flood (2001) points out systemic thinking is a grounding for action research in how it helps construct meaning that resonates with our experience within a systemic world. Hence your research-in-action can benefit from an awareness of and skills in working with interlevel dynamics.

1 (a) Who are the individuals involved in this project? How do I work with them?
     (b) Who are the teams involved in this project? How do I work with them?
     (c) What are the issues between these teams? How do I work at the interteam level?
2 In the teams in the project, what impact are individuals having on the team in which they are members and vice versa?
3 What are the significant patterns of relationships between individuals, teams, the interdepartmental group and the organization that I need to be sensitive to and work with?
	Exercise 9.1
	Applying interlevel dynamics

	Individual	Team	Interdepartmental group	Organization
Individual	▓			
Team		▓		
Interdepartmental group			▓	
Organization				▓

1   Name a change issue with regard to an individual.
2   Now work diagonally along the shaded boxes. How does one level have an impact on the others?
3   Where would you put your energies to advance the progress of the change and heal dysfunctions.

Now:
1   Name a change issue which applies to the whole organization.
2   Work diagonally along the shaded boxes. How does one level have an impact on the others?
3   Develop strategies to implement change at each level.

10 Using Frameworks to Study Organizations in Action

We now turn our attention to the process of making sense of organizational dynamics by presenting some features of organizational diagnosis and the use of frameworks. Organizational dynamics and the use of frameworks are subjects in themselves (Bolman and Deal, 1997; Harrison and Shirom, 1999; Burke, 2002). There are innumerable frameworks which can be found in standard textbooks and in the writings of those authors who have created them. For instance, within the field of business strategy you may be familiar with frameworks which enable you to analyse the competitive nature of an industry or relative position of a firm within an industry. Within marketing, you may draw on frameworks which help position a product or service. In every field and subject area there are frameworks which enable you to make sense of the current situation and predict outcomes. In relation to doing action research in your own organization, we highlight the systems approach and give particular attention to constructs of organizational learning and change. We are not attempting to provide a list of such frameworks, but rather aiming at providing an introduction to their use.

Organizational diagnosis

> We use the term *diagnosis* to refer to investigations that draw on concepts, models, and methods from the behavioural sciences in order to examine an organization's current state and help clients find ways to solve problems or enhance organizational effectiveness.
>
> (Harrison and Shirom, 1999: 7)

Underlying the principle of organizational diagnosis is a notion of organizational health which organizational clinicians are using to compare with the present situation (Schein, 1997). Accordingly, frameworks which postulate key organizational variables and relationships are important diagnostic tools.

Organizational frameworks are presentations of organizations which help categorize data, enhance understanding, interpret data and provide a common shorthand language (Burke, 2002). They typically describe relationships between organizational dynamics, such as purpose, strategy, structure, control systems, information systems, rewards systems and culture, and help organize data into useful categories and point to what areas need attention.

Some guidelines are useful for selecting and using frameworks. Weisbord (1988) advises that frameworks should have four features: that they be simple, fit members' values and highlights things they consider important, validate members' experience by putting recognizable things in a new light and that they suggest practical steps. Burke (2002) provides three guidelines for selecting a framework. One is that you should adopt a framework you understand and with which you feel comfortable. The second is that the framework selected should fit the organization as closely as possible, that it be comprehensive enough to cover as many aspects of the organization as appropriate and be clear enough for members of the organization to grasp. The third is that the framework should be sufficiently comprehensive to enable data gathering and interpretation without omitting key pieces of information. In a word of caution, Burke points out that you may become trapped by your frameworks, so that your way of seeing becomes a way of not seeing. So as an action researcher, you need to critique the frameworks you use.

Systems thinking and practice

A significant contribution to situation analysis is systems thinking and practice. Systems thinking refers to seeing organizations as a whole, made up of interrelated and interdependent parts. The human body is a good example of a system, whereby bones, muscles, tissues and organs perform interdependent and interrelated functions. While we might dissect the body and make an analysis of any particular part, the body's functioning depends on a holistic view of how all the parts work together. Similarly, organizations may be viewed as systems, in which planning, control, structural, technological and behavioural systems are interdependent and inter-related.

Understanding organizations as open systems, that is being dependent on its external environment for its survival, has been well established in organizational theory for many years (Katz and Kahn, 1978). What has received less emphasis is the 'recursive' systems model, which represents organizations as patterns of feedback loops and sequences of interaction which link and integrate elements of a system (Senge, 1990; McCaughan and Palmer, 1994; Haslebo and Nielsen, 2000). In systems thinking, linear cause and effect analysis is replaced by viewing patterns of interaction which mutually influence each other.

'Dynamic complexity' refers to situations where a system is complex, not because of a lot of detail but because of multiple causes and effects over time (Senge, 1990). In situations of dynamic complexity, systems thinking provides a perspective of viewing and understanding how a system is held together by patterns of action and reaction, relationships, meanings and hidden rules and the role of time. In order to inquire into how a system functions, you can engage in systemic questioning (McCaughan and Palmer, 1994):

- *Establishing circuitry*: When A does . . . what does B do? What does A do next?
- *Establishing patterns*: What patterns are evident over time?
- *Exploring meaning*: What are the meanings held in the system? What are the common meanings attributed to events and actions?
- *Exploring covert rules*: What unarticulated and hidden rules govern behaviour?
- *Exploring the time dimensions*: How time delays have an impact on the system.

It is not easy to find answers to questions posed by systemic questioning. Formulation of tentative working explanations as to what is happening in the system – the circuitry, patterns, covert rules, meanings and time – may uncover the dynamic complexity of the system and may involve many iterations of collaborative inquiry before finding explanations which fit.

Systems thinking and action research

Systems thinking and the action research cycle play complementary roles. In a systems approach to action research, tentative explanations are being formed as the story unfolds. These explanations are tentative frames to articulate the elements of the system in order that they may be understood and to consider interventions to change them, where required. A very useful way of formulating systemic explanations is through the use of diagrammatic representation. When cycles of action and their consequences are drawn in a diagram, the patterns of the system may be illuminated. Both the act of attempting to represent the system diagrammatically and the diagram itself are essential elements of the learning process. The very act of drawing the system's diagram is a learning process of explanation formulation and testing (Anderson and Johnson, 1997). In traditional research approaches, intuition is frequently placed against reasoning and considered alien from a research process. In Senge's (1990) view, the systems approach holds the key to integrating intuition and reason, because intuition goes beyond linear thinking to recognize patterns, draw analogies and solve problems creatively.

Change and learning

As change and learning are central to action research, it is important for the action researcher to draw on knowledge of how change and learning take place (Burke, 2002; Schein, 1996b, 1999b). How change and learning take place applies not only to individuals, but also to groups, between groups and to organizations, as we saw in the previous chapter. Change theory has evolved from Lewin's (1948) model that the change process has three stages or sets of issues: being motivated to change, changing, and making the change survive and work. Lewin argues that a system must unlearn before it can relearn and that attention to all three stages are equally critical. Lewin's research and theory of change has been a formative influence on the emergence of the theory and practice of organization development (French and Bell, 1999).

Any action researcher in an organization needs to understand how people in organizations can resist change (Coghlan and McAuliffe, 2003). An important starting place is that resistance is a healthy, self-regulating manifestation which must be respected and taken seriously by the action researcher. Rashford and Coghlan (1994) present two psychological reactions to the initiation of a change. When a change agenda is first presented people may *deny* its relevance. When denial is no longer sustainable it may be replaced by *dodging*, which is an effort at diverting the change. Denial and dodging are natural reactions to a change agenda, especially when it is unexpected. In Rashford and Coghlan's view, they are a prelude to *doing* and *sustaining*, when the change agenda is accepted and implemented.

There are different levels of change and learning which have a particular relevance to action research. From the work of Bateson (1972) and others who have developed his work, a distinction between change or learning which deals with routine issues and that which involves a change of thinking or adoption of a different mental model is typically defined as a distinction between single- and double-loop learning (Argyris and Schon, 1996) and first-, second- or third-order change (Moch and Bartunek, 1990).

First-order change occurs when a specific change is identified and implemented within an existing way of thinking. For example, Bartunek et al. (2000) describe management-led action research in a bank on a problem of communication problems with clients. Through the action research process of participative data gathering, data analysis, feedback and action planning, intervention and evaluation, the named problem was addressed and improvements made.

Second-order change occurs when a first-order change is inadequate and when the change requires lateral thinking and questioning and altering the core assumptions which underlie the situation. In another example, Bartunek et al. describe a manager-led action research project which initially aimed at addressing improving a manufacturing system by increasing volume while maintaining flexibility, as well as enabling automated material control and improved planning. As the data were being analysed, it became evident that these changes would involve creating a radically new way the company did business. Accordingly, through the action research cycle, materials personnel, assemblers, testers and supervisors/managers participated in diagnosis, analysis and feedback resulting in the implementation of a new integrated manufacturing system. Due to the success of this project, a similar methodology was applied to other change projects in the company.

It is realized that sometimes, concrete problems are symptoms of complex attitudinal and cultural problems which must be addressed and that problem resolution involves organizational transformation. This is called *third-order change* which occurs when the members of an organization learn to question their own assumptions and points of view and develop and implement new ones.

Issues may not be obvious. First-order problems may persist unless there is second-order change. A recurrent demand for second-order change may point to the need for the development of third-order skills. Observation of a group at work may yield questions as to what particular behaviours or patterns of behaviour mean. What is critical is that you as the action researcher inquire into those patterns and facilitate the group in surfacing and examining them, rather than making a private interpretation, which is untested and then becomes the basis for action. Taking what is directly observable into the realm of meaning requires skills in inquiry and intervention as we discussed in Chapter 3.

Conclusions

In this chapter we have outlined how you would approach making sense of complex organizational data. We have presented some major themes with respect to how you might go about choosing a framework on which you would base your understanding of organizational data and on the basis of which you would take action.

Making sense has different applications in different contexts where the action research in your own organization is linked to academic accreditation. In a masters programme, such as an MBA or its equivalent, frameworks such as those discussed in this chapter are used to help you see more clearly what is going on and to design appropriate interventions to deal with the issues identified.

In a masters by research and a PhD you go further. In this context, you not only use the frameworks to help you see what is going on and to plan further action, but you also critique and extend theoretical frameworks in order to contribute to theory development.

Exercise 10.1 *Diagnosing your organization*	Take any organizational diagnostic framework from any textbook and apply the boxes and process lines to your own organization. 1　What picture is emerging? 2　What do you need to do to check the picture you have of the organization? 3　Where do you think you need to intervene? 4　How do you justify that diagnosis and intervention selection?

Some useful books which can help you do some systems thinking and mapping are: Senge et al. (1994) and Anderson and Johnson (1997). On a sheet of paper:

1   Describe the issue/problem as you see it.
2   Tell the story.
3   Draw a map of the story: When A said/did . . . What did B do? What did A do next? What was the outcome for C?
4   Connect the process of the story with arrows.
5   Include where you are in the story and what your interests are.
6   Consider any number of explanations of the patterns.
7   Consider any number of interventions which might change the structure of the system, and see how each intervention has different outcomes across the system.

Exercise 10.2
Using systems thinking

11 Writing Your Action Research Dissertation

At the end of the academic-oriented action research project you have to write a dissertation. In non-academic contexts you may write a report or want to write an article or paper. In this chapter we discuss how to structure and present the final version of your dissertation. We assume that you have been writing all through your project as you have written up accounts of events and kept your own personal journal and reflections up to date. It is important that you keep records and notes in real time, close to events so that you have an accurate record of what took place and what you were thinking about them at the time.

As we discussed in Chapter 2, there are two action research projects running concurrently, what Zuber-Skerritt and Perry (2002) call the 'core' action research project and the 'thesis' action research project. Now we are focusing on writing up the 'thesis' action research which is the inquiry-in-action into how the 'core' action research project was designed, implemented and evaluated and how you enacted your role in it and how you now reflect on it.

A dissertation is an academic document and therefore needs to conform to academic requirements around justification of topic and approach, description and defence of rigour in methodology and methods of inquiry, familiarity with existing content and process literature and contribution to knowledge. An action research dissertation is no different, though its presentation and argument differ from traditional presentations.

There are well-established conventions on writing an action research dissertation which are found in such action research manuals as McNiff et al. (1996), Dick (1999) and Stringer (1999). These typically suggest that it be structured to deal with:

- purpose and rationale of the research;
- context;
- methodology and method of inquiry;

- story and outcomes;
- self-reflection and learning of the action researcher;
- reflection on the story in the light of the experience and the theory;
- extrapolation to a broader context and articulation of usable knowledge.

This is not to say that such a structure would necessarily mean that each of these headings has to be a chapter in itself, but rather that these issues be clearly dealt with formally. For example, the story may be spread over several chapters, depending on its length and complexity and the extent of the research project.

Constructing and writing your dissertation

Purpose and rationale of the research

When you present the purpose and rationale of your research you are, in effect, presenting its academic context. This involves stating why the action you have chosen is worth doing and why it is worth studying. The most critical issue for you at the outset of writing an action research dissertation is to make an academic case for what you are doing. This is not just an argument for credibility but a formal effort to locate your work in an academic context.

Context

Context here refers to the social and academic context of the research. There are three context areas: broad general context at global and national level; local organizational/discipline context, that is what is going on in your organization; and then your specific topic area. In action research social context is very important. Therefore you need to describe the organization or community with which you are working. This would include details of the organization, community or group, what it does, some historical background, what its concerns are and what the issues in which you are engaging with it mean and what is intended and hoped for out of the action research project. This description contains not only a presentation of the facts of the organization in its setting but also contains an extensive literature on the setting. For instance, participants undertaking action research in the masters programme in Health Service Management at the University of Dublin typically have a chapter describing general developments in the Irish health system, locating their action research in national strategy and then in developments in their particular discipline or field. More specifically, a nurse undertaking action research in his or her hospital would review some of the literature on hospital management and track changes in theory and practice in that field as the context in which his or her own research takes place. Then a more specific treatment of local issues would be done – the history, the issues confronting service delivery or management and so linking to the rationale for action and for research.

Academic context is also important. Not only are you reviewing the social context of your project, you also review and critique the research that has been done in that context. We refer to this literature as 'outset' literature, that is the literature that you read, discuss and critique at the outset of your research and which helps ground your research in existing work and opens the door to your contribution.

Methodology and method of inquiry

This is your major section on methodology in which you outline and justify your approach. Here you describe your action research approach, methodology and methods of inquiry. Methodology is your philosophical approach; methods describe what you actually did. Accordingly, you need to both articulate your methodology and your methods of inquiry.

As with any research dissertation you'll need to review the theory and practice of your methodology, in this instance action research. This is a matter of providing definitions, some history and its main philosophical tenets. Second, you will also then review the practice of action research in your own field, such as in nursing, education, information systems research, and so on. Third, you will need to describe and review the particular approach within action research that you might be using, particularly if you are using one approach predominantly. Accordingly, for example, you will review and critique the theory and practice of appreciative inquiry, cooperative inquiry, action learning, and so on, as appropriate.

Regarding methodology, you need to convey that you are using a normal and natural research paradigm with a long tradition and adequate rigour which is suitable for the project on which you have worked. As Dick (1999) very usefully points out, it is important to argue positively for your approach, rather than to criticize negatively the limitations of other approaches. As we presented in the earlier chapters, the action research literature provides extensive justification of how action research is scientific and rigorous.

While all research demands rigour, action research has to demonstrate its rigour more particularly. This is because in action research you typically start out with a fuzzy question, are fuzzy about your methodology in the initial stages and have fuzzy answers in the early stages. As the project develops your methods and answers become less fuzzy and so your questions become less fuzzy. This progression from fuzziness to clarity is the essence of the spirals of action research cycles (Gummesson, 2000). Accordingly, you need to demonstrate clearly the procedures you have used to achieve rigour and defend them. As Dick (1999) emphasizes, this means that you show:

- your use of action research learning cycles;
- how you accessed multiple data sources to provide contradictory and confirming interpretations;
- evidence of how you have challenged and tested your own assumptions and interpretations continuously throughout the project;
- how your interpretations and outcomes are challenged, supported or disconfirmed from existing literature.

As we discussed in Chapter 1, it is important to be explicit about how you have tried to ensure quality. In terms of Reason and Bradbury's (2001) choice points how can this study be judged in terms of:

- being explicitly both aimed at and grounded in the world of practice?
- being explicitly and actively participative: research *with*, *for* and *by* people rather than *on* people?
- drawing on a wide range of ways of knowing – including intuitive, experiential, presentational as well as conceptual – and link these appropriately to form theory?
- being worthy of the term significant?
- emerging towards a new and enduring infrastructure?

As Reason (2003) points out your research cannot rate equally highly at all of these, so he argues that as an action researcher you need to be aware that these are choice points. Accordingly, you can select which ones you want to be judged against and make them clear and transparent.

In terms of Shani and Pasmore's (1985) complete theory of action research the quality of your project rests on how you have presented:

- context;
- quality of relationships;
- quality of the action research process itself;
- outcomes.

In your section on methods you describe how you are doing action research. Methods of inquiry refer to the content and process issues of how you framed and selected the issue, built participation and support, how you accessed and generated data, how you recorded data. Notes and minutes of meetings, journal, where and how you used observation, interviews or survey instruments, how you engaged others in the action research cycles of implementing the project, how you dealt with political and ethical dimensions presented in Chapter 6, particularly with regard to reflective learning, and so on, are all pertinent issues.

Story and outcomes

The heart of the dissertation is the story of what took place. At the initial stages you are likely to construct the story around a chronological narrative and structure it in terms of significant time periods or particular projects. So at the draft stages you might have narratives which cover periods of time or particular projects. This is an important structure to follow as it enables you to get the story down on paper in a logical sequence. The next stage of writing the story is to reflect on it and see what themes emerge. Then you may find that you are surfacing images or themes for the time periods or projects which capture your sense of the meaning of the project and lead you to a synthesis.

Action researchers are often surprised at what happens during the writing of a dissertation. They think that it is simply a mechanical task of writing up what is in their notes and files. Experience shows that the writing up period is a whole new learning experience. It is where synthesis and integration take place. From what hitherto have been isolated masses of details of meetings, events and organizational data, notes on scraps of paper and disks, notes from books and articles, a new reality emerges. Things begin to make sense and meanings form. For many researchers, this is the time they realize what they have been doing all along.

Writing the story is key to synthesis. You are likely to have far more detail than you need or can use. Therefore, as you begin to select what to include and exclude, you are beginning to form a view of what is important in the story. You are at the next stage of reflective practice and indeed of action research itself. The writing project becomes an action research project as you engage in cycles of drafting and revising, seeking comments from your supervisor, reflecting, understanding how what you have written fits into the whole, and then formulating conclusions (Zuber-Skerritt and Perry, 2002). It is far from being the mechanical task of writing up your notes that you might have thought.

A critical issue in presenting the story is to distinguish the events which took place, about which there is no dispute, and the meanings attributed to these events. It is important to present separately the basic story as if it were a news bulletin, as if a video camera had recorded what had taken place. This form of presentation gives the evidence in a factual and neutral manner. Your view of these events and your theorizing as to what they mean should not be mixed in with the telling of the story. This should come later, perhaps at the end of the chapter or the end of a particular phase of the story. By separating the story from its sense-making, and by clearly stating which is story and which is sense-making, you are demonstrating how you are applying methodological rigour to your approach. Combining narrative and sense-making leaves you open to the charge of biased story-telling and makes it difficult for readers to evaluate your work.

	Box 11.1 Reflecting in public
A useful technique for using your own reflections as you are telling the story is to insert a box at periodic intervals, giving your own reflections on what you have just recounted. Here you can reflect in public, show your train of thought and share what you plan to do next and why.	

This technique provides a mechanism for having accounts of your own reactions, interpretations and action planning alongside factual narrative in a way that doesn't confuse the two. The reader then can see what is happening in the story and then in the boxes read what you are thinking and how you are interpreting the situation as it unfolds and then follow the logic of your actions. This is a tool for inserting first-person narrative alongside the second-person narrative.

In an action research dissertation your account of your sense-making often takes three forms. One is where you make sense of particular events within the narrative as it progresses. The technique described in Box 11.1 is one such form. The second form is where at the end of a chapter or section you may present how you make sense of that event. You do that clearly so that the reader knows what you are doing and goes back to the story to see how your interpretations make sense. It is important that your sense-making sections are not too far from the story narrative. If you leave all your sense-making to chapters at the end, particularly in a doctoral dissertation, it makes it difficult for the reader to remember to what you are referring. The third form sense-making takes is that you have a general chapter towards the end of the dissertation which integrates the more specific interpretations you have made and provides an overview of your sense-making of the whole story and links it back to the purpose of the research, the context and the contribution to actionable knowledge.

It is at this stage that you may have to engage in a further content literature review. This is what we call 'emergent' literature. As you are progressing through the story and making sense of the story you will find that you are being drawn into more specific or even new areas of content, whose literature you now need to read and review. In action research projects, specific relevant content areas emerge as the project progresses, so you often do not quite know what the focus of your synthesis is until the project is well in progress. Content literature becomes more focused through the story and directly relates to what is being framed in the story. A participant in the masters programme in Health Service Management at the University of Dublin found that as her action research progressed team dynamics became central so she read books and articles on teamwork and stages of team development to help her make sense of what was going on in her team and to assist her in her team role in leading the project. This was an area of literature that emerged in her project and could not have been anticipated at the outset.

Self-reflection and learning of the action researcher

An important part of the action research dissertation is your reflection on your own learning. As you have been intervening in the organizational system over the period of the action research project, you need to articulate what you have learned, not only about the system you have been working to change, but about yourself as an action researcher. The project may have challenged many of your assumptions, attitudes, skills and existing organizational relationships. Many of these points of learning have been expressed in the boxes, discussed above, which try to capture your reflection in action. This first-person material is important as it contributes to the integration of the three voices – first, second and third.

Winter (1989) argues that your presentation should reflect your own process of learning and not be a judgement of others. He makes the relevant point that you should avoid making commentaries which place you as the researcher in the superior role of one whose analysis of other people's words show that you understand what took place, while they do not. He suggests that your commentary should place you at risk, as the single voice of the author in a context where many people participated in the work.

One particular dilemma that action researchers face in writing their reports is whether to use the personal first-person or the impersonal third-person narrative style when referring to themselves as the researcher or author. There is no consensus. Krim (1988) and Holian (1999) use the personal 'I' throughout; Goode and Bartunek (1990) and Coghlan (1996) refer to the impersonal 'the consultant'. A useful guideline in our experience is that if the report contains extensive reflection on the personal learning of the author-researcher as agent of the action in the story (as instanced by Krim), then the first-person narrative adds a considerable strength to the published report. Third-person narrative gives a sense of objectivity, while using the first-person demands that the distinction between the story's narrative and the researcher's interpretation and sense-making be very clearly distinct.

Reflection on the story in the light of the experience and the theory

One of the most common criticisms of published action research is that it lacks theory. In other words, action research accounts tell a story but do not address issues of emergent theory and so contribute to knowledge. Accordingly, your action research project needs to apply some established theory or extend or develop theory. The scope of the academic project, whether masters or doctorate, is an important determinant of what is to be expected in this regard.

If you are a participant in a masters programme engaging in pragmatic action research, such as an action-oriented MBA programme, you use frameworks to make sense of what is going on. You may be drawing on frameworks which help you make sense of an industry analysis, performance of the firm and the like. Your use of these frameworks aligns the story to the theory, and through this alignment you demonstrate your understanding of the theory and its application.

If you are engaged in a more research-oriented programme, such as a masters by research or a doctorate, you are not only aligning the story with theory, but also extending that theory or developing it. This extension is an inductive process, coming out of your meta learning of reflecting on the implementation of the action research cycles with the members of the systems as they enact the action research project. This extension or development of existing theory may be in content, as instanced in Coghlan's (1996) application of interlevel dynamics to large system change in a longitudinal study, or process, as in Krim's (1988) developmental action inquiry approach to learning in a political environment.

Extrapolation to a broader context and articulation of usable knowledge

As a consequence of your reflection on the story and articulation of usable knowledge, you need to articulate how your research project can be extrapolated to a wider context. Such an extrapolation answers the 'so what?' question in relation to your research and completes the agenda that good research is for me, for us and for them, that is, it integrates first-, second- and third-person research. This section is answering the question, 'Why should anyone who has not been involved directly in my research be interested in it?'

Action research projects are situation specific and do not aim to create universal knowledge. At the same time, extrapolation from a local situation to more general situations is important. As an action researcher you are not claiming that every organization will behave as the one you have studied. But you can focus on some significant factors, consideration of which is useful for other organizations, perhaps like organizations or organizations undergoing similar types of change processes.

For readers whose action research is directed at both a practical organizational outcome and an academic assessment, it may be useful for you to produce two documents. Organizational readers tend to be interested primarily in the story and its analysis, and less interested in academic citations, critiques of methodology, literature reviews and discussions of theoretical differences between schools of thought, which are central to an academic dissertation. For the organizational readers, the researcher may produce a report which contains the core story and its analysis, omitting the academic requirements.

Dissemination

Dissemination of action research occurs in ways similar to all forms of research dissemination. A dissertation is held in a library, with its abstract circulated on abstract indexes. Articles and papers may be submitted to journals and books. Throughout this book we have referenced many such published accounts.

Political sensitivities are typically critical issues in the writing of the research report and its dissemination. The content of the report may contain classified material or data of interest to competitors. Individual actors may be identifiable and their reported role in the events of the story may not be complimentary. Conventions relating to disguising the identity of the case and the actors may be applied. Krim (1988) does not identify the city hall in which his research took place and probably, for most readers, its identity is irrelevant and subordinate to the theme and methodology of the research.

A particular application of action research dissemination involves those who have participated as co-researchers in the project. You may have a moral obligation to involve them in the conclusions and the report. In terms of communicating your analysis back to the organization, Nielsen and Repstad (1992) advise:

- Do not promise greater anonymity than you can keep.
- Take actors' analyses seriously.
- Point to potential solutions.
- Take the opportunity to discuss with as many as possible.

Conclusions

Writing the action research dissertation is an act of learning and is itself an action research project. During the writing of the dissertation you draw together the complexities of all your data and engage in a sense-making activity that integrates your own personal learning as well as what took place in the system in which you worked. Telling the story, making sense of it, applying a rigorous methodology to that sense-making are directed towards the generation of useful knowledge which must produce outcomes which are of value to others.

In Conclusion

In this book we have explored a subject which is receiving more attention year by year, and continues to represent very common practice in post-experience masters and doctoral programmes within business education, healthcare, social work and third sector organizations.

Action research is about undertaking action and studying that action as it takes place. It is about improving practice through intervention, and demands rigorous preparation, planning, action, attention to process, reflection, replanning and validating claims to learning and theory generation. It is collaborative, involving interacting with others. We have focused on the dynamics of how this might be done when the action research is being undertaken in the organization of the action researcher, who is both aiming at achieving personal goals from the project and contributing to the organization. We drew on the image, adapted from Weisbord, of the actor–director in the act of making a film. Film-making involves creating a script whereby the story of the movie is enacted by people in interaction with one another over time. The actor–director engages in both acting in the film and standing back to study how the shots are being taken, how the actors are performing and deciding how subsequent shots need to be set up.

We began our exploration by understanding the basic tenets of action research and unravelling the multiple forms it takes. Then we explored the three core foundational elements: how action research works through (a) the spirals of cycles of diagnosing, planning, taking and evaluating action, and the meta cycle of content, process and premise reflection; (b) how the individual researcher learns in action; and (c) how the whole process is genuinely collaborative. In all this the critical skills are introspective reflection and, when engaging with others, combining advocacy with inquiry. While many of the issues of any research project pertain to researching your own organization, the particular challenges posed by researching your own organization are around managing the closeness–distance tension in preunderstanding and in managing role duality, and around managing the politics in order that you have a future in the organization when the research is completed.

Nielsen and Repstad (1993) describe the notion of researching your own organization in terms of a journey from nearness to distance and back and provide some practical advice. In terms of maintaining distance, they advise that you be aware of your preconceived ideas and prejudices about the organization and find rational theories to explain the organization as a way of distancing yourself. They suggest that you perform the role of devil's advocate by finding alternative theories which contradict the rational theories you have selected to explain the organization by engaging in dialogue with other members of the organization. In their view, you need to consider seriously the prevailing explanation of organizational problems, which might reflect analyses of symptoms. These would typically be: (a) the scapegoat syndrome − 'who is to blame'; (b) too little information − 'if only we had more'; and (c) too few resources − 'if only we had more'.

What you can do in an action research project in your own organization depends on the formal and psychological contract you have with the system on its commitment to learning in action juxtaposed with yours. This is critical to the nature of the project you can undertake. You draw on your preunderstanding of the organization and how you can manage the twin roles of your regular organizational role with the researcher role. With that foundation we explored some important and useful issues − managing organizational politics, framing and selecting a project, implementing it and, finally, writing an action research dissertation.

For some readers doing action research in their own organizations is an exciting, demanding and invigorating prospect which will contribute considerably to their own learning and help their career development. For others it may seem daunting with a high potential for self-destruction. In the words of Brookfield (1994) it smacks of impostorship, cultural suicide, lost innocence, road running and community. Can you survive doing action research in your own organization? Shepard (1997) provides a few rules of thumb for change agents which are also useful for insider action researchers.

1   *Stay alive*. Care for yourself. Keep a life outside of the project so as to be able to turn yourself on and off. Stay in touch with the purpose of the project and go with the flow.
2   *Start where the system is*. Have empathy with the system and the people in it, particularly as it will not like being 'diagnosed'.
3   *Never work uphill*. Keep working at collaboration and work in the most promising arena.
4   *Innovation requires a good idea, initiative and a few friends*. Find the people who are ready to work on the project and get them working together.

5 *Load experiments with success.* Work at building success steps along the way.
6 *Light many fires.* Remember the notion of systems. Any part of a system is the way it is because of how the rest of the system is. As you work towards change in one part, other parts will push the system back to the way it was. Understand the interdependencies among subsystems and keep movement going in as many of them as you can.
7 *Keep an optimistic bias.* Stay focused on vision and desired outcomes.
8 *Capture the moment.* Stay in tune with yourself and the situation.

Friedman (2001b) suggests four attributes: be proactive and reflective; be critical and committed; be independent and work well with others; and have aspirations and be realistic about limits. With these in mind we are confident that not only can you survive doing action research in your own organization, but you can flourish and be successful.

References

Adler, P.A. and Adler, P. (1987) *Membership Roles in Field Research*. Thousand Oaks, CA: Sage.

Adler, N., Shani, A.B. (Rami) and Styhre, A. (2004) *Collaborative Research in Organizations*. Thousand Oaks, CA: Sage.

Alvesson, M. (1999) 'Methodology for close up studies – Struggling with closeness and closure', Institute of Economic Research Working Paper, 1999/4, Lund: University of Lund.

Alvesson, M. and Skoldberg, K. (2000) *Reflexive Methodology: New Vistas for Qualitative Research*. Thousand Oaks, CA: Sage.

Anderson, G., Herr, K. and Nihlen, A. (1994) *Studying your Own School*. Thousand Oaks, CA: Corwin.

Anderson, V. and Johnson, L. (1997) *Systems Thinking Basics: From Concepts to Causal Loops*. Cambridge, MA: Pegasus.

Argyris, C. (1990) *Overcoming Organizational Defenses*. Boston, MA: Allyn and Bacon.

Argyris, C. (1993) *Knowledge for Action*. San Francisco, CA: Jossey-Bass.

Argyris, C. (1999) *On Organizational Learning*, 2nd edition. Oxford: Blackwell.

Argyris, C. (2003) 'Actionable knowledge', in T. Tsoukas and C. Knudsen (eds), *The Oxford Handbook of Organization Theory*. Oxford: Oxford University Press. pp. 423–52.

Argyris, C. (2004) *Reasons and Rationalizations: The Limits to Organizational Knowledge*. New York: Oxford University Press.

Argyris, C. and Schon, D. (1996) *Organizational Learning II*. Reading, MA: Addison-Wesley.

Argyris, C., Putnam, R. and Smith, D. (1985) *Action Science*. San Francisco, CA: Jossey-Bass.

Ashforth, B., Kreiner, G. and Fugate, M. (2000) 'All in a day's work: Boundaries and micro role transitions', *Academy of Management Review*, 25 (3): 472–91.

Atwal, A. (2003) 'Getting the evidence into practice: The challenges and successes of action research', *British Journal of Occupational Therapy*, 65 (7): 335–41.

Bartunek, J.M. (1988) 'The dynamics of personal and organizational reframing', in R. Quinn and K. Cameron (eds), *Paradox and Transformation: Toward a Theory of Change in Organizations and Management*. Cambridge, MA: Ballinger. pp. 137–62.

Bartunek, J.M. (2003) *Organizational and Educational Change: The Life and Role of a Change Agent Group*. Mahwah, NJ: Erblaum.

Bartunek, J.M. and Louis, M.R. (1996) *Insider/Outsider Team Research*. Thousand Oaks, CA: Sage.

Bartunek, J.M., Crosta, T.E., Dame, R.F. and LeLacheur, D.F. (2000) 'Managers and project leaders conducting their own action research interventions', in R.T. Golembiewski (ed.), *Handbook of Organizational Consultation*, 2nd edition. New York: Marcel Dekker. pp. 59–70.

Baskerville, R. and Pries-Heje, J. (1999) 'Grounded action research: A method for understanding IT in practice', *Accounting Management and Information Technology*, 9: 1–23.

Bateson, G. (1972) *Steps to an Ecology of Mind*. San Francisco, CA: Ballantine.

Beckhard, R. (1997) *Agent of Change, My Life, My Work*. San Francisco, CA: Jossey-Bass.

Beckhard, R. and Harris, R. (1987) *Organizational Transitions: Managing Complex Change*, 2nd edition. Reading, MA: Addison-Wesley.

Beckhard, R. and Pritchard, W. (1992) *Changing the Essence: The Art of Creating and Leading Fundamental Change in Organizations*. San Francisco, CA: Jossey-Bass.

Bentz, V.M. and Shapiro J.J. (1998) *Mindful Inquiry in Social Research*. Thousand Oaks, CA: Sage.

Bolman, D. and Deal, T. (1997) *Reframing Organizations*, 2nd edition. San Francisco, CA: Jossey-Bass.

Bourdieu, P. (1990) *The Logic of Practice*. Cambridge: Polity Press.

Bray, J., Lee, J., Smith, L. and Yorks, L. (2000). *Collaborative Inquiry in Practice*. Thousand Oaks, CA: Sage.

Brookfield, S. (1994) 'Tales from the dark side: A phenomenography of adult critical reflection, *International Journal of Lifelong Education*, 13 (3): 203–16.

Brooks, A. and Watkins, K.E. (1994) *The Emerging Power of Action Inquiry Technologies*. San Francisco, CA: Jossey-Bass.

Buchanan, D. and Badham, R. (1999) *Power, Politics and Organizational Change: Winning the Turf Game*. London: Sage.

Buchanan, D. and Boddy, D. (1992) *The Expertise of the Change Agent*. London: Prentice Hall.

Burke, W.W. (2002) *Organization Change: Theory and Practice*. Thousand Oaks, CA: Sage.

Chandler, D. and Torbert, W.R. (2003) 'Transforming inquiry and action: Interweaving 27 flavors of action research', *Action Research*, 1 (2): 133–52.

Chisholm, R.F. (1998) *Developing Network Organizations*. Reading, MA: Addison-Wesley.

Chisholm, R. (2001) 'Action research to develop an interorganizational network', in P. Reason and H. Bradbury (eds), *Handbook of Action Research*. London: Sage. pp. 324–32.

Church, A., Gilbert, M., Oliver, D., Paquet, K. and Surface, C. (2001) 'The role of technology in organization development and change', in A. Benson and S. Johnson (eds), *Advances in Developing Human Resources Development and Learning Technologies in HRD*, special issue, 4 (4): 493–511.

Coch, L. and French, J.R.P. (1948) 'Overcoming resistance to change', *Human Relations*, 1: 512–32.

Coghlan, D. (1993) 'Learning from emotions through journaling', *Journal of Management Education*, 17 (1): 90–4.

Coghlan, D. (1996) 'Mapping the progress of change through organizational levels: The example of a religious order', in R. Woodman and W. Pasmore (eds*), Research in Organizational Change and Development*, vol. 9. Greenwich, CT: JAI. pp. 123–50.

Coghlan, D. (1997) 'Organizational learning as a dynamic interlevel process', in M.A. Rahim, R.T. Golembiewski and L.E. Pate (eds), *Current Topics in Management,* vol. 2. Greenwich, CT: JAI. pp. 27–44.

Coghlan, D. (2002) 'Interlevel dynamics in systemic action research', *Systemic Practice and Action Research*, 15 (4): 273–83.

Coghlan, D. (2003) 'Practitioner research for organizational knowledge: Mechanistic and organistic-oriented approaches to insider action research', *Management Learning*, 34 (4): 451–63.

Coghlan, D. and Casey, M. (2001) 'Action research from the inside: Issues and challenges in doing action research in your own hospital', *Journal of Advanced Nursing*, 35: 674–82.

Coghlan, D. and Coughlan, P. (2003) 'Acquiring the capacity for operational improvement: An action research opportunity', *Human Resource Planning*, 26 (2): 30–8.

Coghlan, D. and McAuliffe, E. (2003) *Changing Healthcare Organizations*. Dublin: Blackhall.

Coghlan, D. and McDonagh, J. (2001) 'Research and practice in IT-related change: The case for clinical inquiry', in R. Woodman, and W. Pasmore (eds), *Research in Organizational Change and Development*, vol. 13. Greenwich, CT: JAI. pp. 195–211.

Coghlan, D. and Rashford, N.S. (1990) 'Uncovering and dealing with organizational distortions', *Journal of Managerial Psychology*, 5 (3): 17–21.

Coghlan, D., Dromgoole, T., Joynt, P. and Sorensen, P. (2004) *Managers Learning in Action: Research, Learning and Education*. London: Routledge.

Cooklin, A. (ed.) (1999) *Changing Organizations: Clinicians as Agents of Change*. London: Karnac.

Cooper, J. and Hewison, A. (2002) 'Implementing audit in palliative care: An action research approach', *Journal of Advanced Nursing*, 39: 360–9.

Cooperrider, D.L. and Srivastva, S. (1987) 'Appreciative inquiry in organizational life', in R. Woodman, and W. Pasmore (eds), *Research in Organizational Change and Development*, vol. 1. Greenwich, CT: JAI. pp. 129–69.

Cooperrider, D.L., Sorensen, P.F., Whitney, D. and Yaeger, T.F. (eds) (2000) *Appreciative Inquiry: Rethinking Organization Toward a Positive Theory of Change*. Champaign, IL: Stipes.

Cooperrider, D.L., Whitney, D. and Stavros, J. (2003) *Appreciative Inquiry Handbook*. Bedford Heights, OH: Lakeshore Communications.

Cornell, A.W. (1996) *The Power of Focusing*. Oakland, CA: New Harbinger Publications.

Coughlan, P. and Coghlan, D. (2002) 'Action research for operations management', *International Journal of Operations and Production Management*, 22 (2): 220–40.

Cunningham, J.B. (1993) *Action Research and Organization Development.* Westport, CT: Praeger.

Darling, M. and Parry, C. (2000) *From Post-Mortem to Living Practice: An In-depth Study of the Evolution of the After Action Review.* Boston, MA: Signet.

Deane, C. (2004) 'Learning to change', in D. Coghlan, T. Dromgoole, P. Joynt and P. Sorensen (eds), *Managers Learning in Action: Research, Learning and Education.* London: Routledge. pp.10–23.

de Guerre, D. (2002) 'Doing action research in one's own organization: An ongoing conversation over time', *Systemic Practice and Action Research*, 15 (4): 331–49.

Dick, B. (1999) 'You want to do an action research thesis?' http://www.scu.edu.au/schools/sawd/arr/arth/arthesis.html

Dickens, L. and Watkins, K. (1999) 'Action research: Rethinking Lewin', *Management Learning*, 30 (2): 127–40.

Dilworth, L. and Willis, V. (2003) *Action Learning: Images and Pathways.* Malabar, FL: Krieger.

Dutton, J.E. and Duncan, R.B. (1987) 'The creation of momentum for change through the process of strategic issue diagnosis', *Strategic Management Journal*, 8: 279–95.

Dutton, J.E. and Jackson, S.E. (1987) 'Categorizing strategic issues: Links to organizational action', *Academy of Management Review*, 12 (1): 76–90.

Dutton, J.E. and Ottensmeyer, E. (1987) 'Strategic issues management systems: Forms, functions and contexts', *Academy of Management Review*, 12 (2): 355–65.

Dutton, J.E., Fahey, L. and Narayanan, V.K. (1983) 'Toward understanding strategic issue diagnosis', *Strategic Management Journal,* 4: 307–23.

Eden, C. and Huxham, C. (1996) 'Action research for the study of organizations', in S.R. Clegg, C. Hardy and W.R. Nord (eds.), *Handbook of Organization Studies.* Thousand Oaks, CA: Sage. pp. 526–42

Eikeland, O. and Finstrud, H. (1995) *Research in Action.* Oslo: The Work Research Institute.

Elden, M. and Chisholm, R.F. (1993) 'Emerging varieties of action research: Introduction to the special issue', *Human Relations*, 46 (2): 121–41.

Elizur, Y. (1999) '"Inside" consultation through self-differentiation: Stimulating organization development in the IDF's care of intractable, war-related, traumatic disorders', in A. Cooklin (ed.), *Changing Organizations: Clinicians as Agents of Change.* London: Karnac. pp. 141–68.

Elliot, J. (1991) *Action Research for Educational Change.* Milton Keynes: Open University.

Evans, M. (1997) 'An action research enquiry into reflection in action as part of my role as a deputy headteacher', PhD thesis: Kingston University. http://www.bath.ac.uk/-edsajw/moyra.html

Evered, M. and Louis, M.R. (1981) 'Alternative perspectives in the organizational sciences: "Inquiry from the inside" and "inquiry from the outside"', *Academy of*

Management Review, 6: 385–95.

Fals-Borda, O. (2001) 'Participatory (action) research in social theory: Origins and challenges', in P. Reason and H. Bradbury (eds), *Handbook of Action Research.* London: Sage. pp. 27–37.

Ferguson, P. and Ferguson, B. (2001) 'Shooting oneself in the foot: An investigation of some issues in conducting insider research', Paper presented at 24th HERDSA conference, Newcastle, Australia.

Fisher, D., Rooke, D. and Torbert, B. (2000) *Personal and Organizational Transformations through Action Inquiry.* Boston, MA: Edge\work Press.

Fisher, R. and Ury, W. (1986) *Getting to Yes.* London: Business Books.

Flood, R. (2001) 'The relationship of "systems thinking" to action research', in P. Reason and H. Bradbury (eds), *Handbook of Action Research.* London: Sage. pp. 133–45.

Flyvbjerg, B. (2001) *Making Social Science Matter.* Cambridge: Cambridge University Press.

Foster, M. (1972) 'An introduction to the theory and practice of action research in work organizations', *Human Relations,* 25 (6): 529–56.

French, W. and Bell, C. (1999) *Organization Development: Behavioral Science Interventions for Organization Improvement,* 6th edition. Englewood Cliffs, NJ: Prentice-Hall.

Friedman, V. (2001a) 'Action science: Creating communities of inquiry in communities of practice', in P. Reason and H. Bradbury (eds), *Handbook of Action Research.* London: Sage. pp. 159–70.

Friedman, V. (2001b) 'The individual as agent of organizational learning', in M. Dierkes, J. Child, I. Nonaka and A. Berthoin Antal (eds), *Handbook of Organizational Learning.* Oxford: Oxford University Press. pp 398–414.

Frohman, A.L. (1997) 'Igniting organizational change from below: The power of personal initiative', *Organizational Dynamics,* Winter: 39–53.

Frost, P. and Robinson, S. (1999) 'The toxic handler: Organizational hero – and casualty', *Harvard Business Review,* July–August: 97–106.

Gendlin, E. (1981) *Focusing.* New York: Bantam.

Gibbon, B. and Little, V. (1995) 'Improving stroke care through action research', *Journal of Clinical Nursing,* 4: 93–100.

Golembiewski, R. (1998) 'Appreciating appreciative inquiry: Diagnosis and perspectives on how to do better', in R. Woodman and W. Pasmore (eds), *Research in Organizational Change and Development,* vol. 11. Greenwich, CT: JAI. pp. 1–45.

Goode, L.M., and Bartunek, J.M. (1990) 'Action research in an underbounded setting', *Consultation,* 9 (3): 209–28.

Gorinski, R. and Ferguson, P. (1997) '(Ex)changing experiences of insider research', NZARE conference. Auckland, New Zealand.

Gosling, J. and Ashton, D. (1994) 'Action learning and academic qualifications', *Management Learning,* 25 (2): 263–74.

Greenwood, D. and Levin, M. (1998) *Introduction to Action Research.* Thousand Oaks, CA: Sage.

Greiner, L.E, and Schein, V.E (1988) *Power and Organization Development.*

Reading, MA: Addison-Wesley.

Gummesson, E. (2000) *Qualitative Methods in Management Research*, 2nd edition. Thousand Oaks, CA: Sage.

Gustavsen, B. (1992) *Dialogue and Development*. Assen: Von Gorcum.

Gustavsen, B. (2001) 'Theory and practice: The mediating discourse', in P. Reason and H. Bradbury (eds), *Handbook of Action Research*. London: Sage. pp. 17–26.

Gustavsen, D. and Englestad, P. (1986) 'The design of conferences and the evolving role of democratic dialogue in changing working life', *Human Relations*, 39: 101–16.

Harrison, M. and Shirom, A. (1999) *Organizational Diagnosis and Assessment: Bridging Theory and Practice*. Thousand Oaks, CA: Sage.

Hart, E. and Bond, M. (1995) *Action Research for Health and Social Care: A Guide to Practice*. Milton Keynes: Open University.

Haslebo, G. and Nielsen, K.S. (2000) *Systems and Meaning: Consulting in Organizations*. London: Karnac.

Heron, J. (1996) *Cooperative Inquiry*. London: Sage.

Heron, J. and Reason, P. (2001) 'The practice of cooperative inquiry: Research "with" rather than "on" people', in P. Reason and H. Bradbury (eds), *Handbook of Action Research*. London: Sage. pp. 179–88.

Heslop, L., Elsom, S. and Parker, N. (2000) 'Improving continuity of patient care across psychiatric emergency services: Combining patient data with a participatory action research framework', *Journal of Advanced Nursing*, 31: 135–43.

Hill, M.R. (1993) *Archival Strategies and Techniques*. Thousand Oaks, CA: Sage.

Holian, R. (1999) 'Doing action research in my own organization: Ethical dilemmas, hopes and triumphs', *Action Research International*, Paper 3. http://www.scu.edu.au/schools/sawd/ari/ari/holian.html

Holley, E. (1997) 'How do I as a teacher-researcher contribute to the development of a living educational theory through an exploration of my values in my professional practice?' M.Phil Thesis, University of Bath. http://www.bath.ac.uk/-edsajw/erica.html

Holman, P. and Devane, T. (1999) *The Change Handbook: Group Methods for Shaping the Future*. San Francisco, CA: Berrett-Koehler.

Homa, P. (1998) 'Re-engineering the Leicester Royal Infirmary healthcare process.' Unpublished Ph.D. thesis, Henley Management College and Brunel University.

Hyrkas, K. (1997) 'Can action research be applied in developing clinical teaching?', *Journal of Advanced, Nursing*, 25: 801–8.

Jarvis, P. (1999) *The Practitioner-Researcher*. San Francisco, CA: Jossey-Bass.

Johnson, P. and Duberley, J. (2000) *Understanding Management Research*. London: Sage.

Kakabadse, A. (1991) 'Politics and ethics in action research', in N. Craig Smith and P. Dainty (eds), *The Management Research Handbook*. London: Routledge. pp. 289–99.

Kaplan, R.S (1998) 'Innovation action research: Creating new management theory and practice', *Journal of Management Accounting Research*, 10: 89–118.

Katz, D. and Kahn, R.L. (1978) *The Social Psychology of Organizations*, 2nd edition. New York: McGraw-Hill.

Kelly, D. and Simpson, S. (2001) 'Action research in action: Reflections on a project to introduce clinical practice facilitators to an acute hospital setting', *Journal of Advanced Nursing*, 33: 652–9.

Kilgour, C. and Fleming, V. (2000) 'An action research inquiry into a health visitor programme for parents of pre-school children with behavioural problems', *Journal of Advanced Nursing*, 32: 689–713.

Kleiner, A. and Roth, G. (1997) 'How to make experience your company's best teacher', *Harvard Business Review,* September–October: 172–7.

Kleiner, A. and Roth, G. (2000) *Oil Change*. New York: Oxford University Press.

Kolb, D. (1984) *Experiential Learning*. Englewood Cliffs, NJ: Prentice-Hall.

Kotter, J. (1985) *Power and Influence: Beyond Formal Authority.* New York: Free Press.

Krim, R. (1988) 'Managing to learn: Action inquiry in city hall', P. Reason (ed.), *Human Inquiry in Action.* London: Sage. pp. 144–62.

Lauri, S. and Sainio, C. (1998) 'Developing the nursing care of breast cancer patients: An action research approach', *Journal of Clinical Nursing*, 7: 424–32.

Lewin, K. (1946) 'Action research and minority problems', in K. Lewin, *Resolving Social Conflicts: Selected Papers on Group Dynamics*. G. Lewin (ed.) reprinted 1997, Washington, DC: American Psychological Association. pp 144–54.

Lewin, K. (1948) 'Group decision and social change', reprinted in M. Gold (ed.) (1999) *The Complete Social Scientist: A Kurt Lewin Reader.* Washington, DC: American Psychological Association. pp. 265–84.

Lippitt, R. (1979) 'Kurt Lewin, action research and planned change', paper provided by the author.

Ludema, J., Cooperrider, D.L. and Barrett, F. (2001) 'Appreciative inquiry: The power of the unconditional positive question', in P. Reason and H. Bradbury (eds), *Handbook of Action Research*. London: Sage. pp. 189–99.

Ludema, J., Whitney, D., Mohr, B. and Griffin, T. (2003) *The Appreciative Inquiry Summit*. San Francisco, CA: Berrett-Kohler.

Lynch, K. (1999) 'Equality studies, the academy and the role of research in emancipatory social change', *Economic and Social Review*, 30 (1): 41–69.

McCaughan, N. and Palmer, B. (1994) *Systems Thinking for Harassed Managers*. London: Karnac.

McElroy, A., Corben, V and McLeish, K. (1995) 'Developing care plan documentation: An action research project', *Journal of Advanced Nursing*, 23: 193–9.

McGill, I. and Brockbank, A. (2004) *The Action Learning Handbook*. London: RoutledgeFalmer.

McMullan, W. and Cahoon, A. (1979) 'Integrating abstract conceptualizing with experiential learning', *Academy of Management Review*, 4 (3): 453–8.

McNiff, J., Lomax, P. and Whitehead, J. (1996) *You and Your Action Research Project*. London: Routledge.

Marrow, A.J. (1969) *The Practical Theorist*. New York: Basic Books.

Marshall, J. (1995) *Women Managers Moving On*. London: Routledge.

Marshall, J. (1999) 'Living life as inquiry', *Systemic Practice and Action Research*, 12 (2): 155–71.

Marshall, J. (2001) 'Self-reflective inquiry practices', in P. Reason and H. Bradbury (eds), *Handbook of Action Research*. London: Sage. pp. 433–9.

Martin, A. (2001) 'Large group interventions as action research', in P. Reason and H. Bradbury (eds), *Handbook of Action Research*, London: Sage. pp. 200–8.

Meehan, C. and Coghlan, D. (forthcoming) 'Managers as healing agents: A cooperative inquiry approach', *Systemic Practice and Action Research*.

Meyerson, D. (2001) *Tempered Radicals: How People use Difference to Inspire Change at Work*. Boston, MA: Harvard Business School Press.

Mezirow, J. (1991) *Transformative Dimensions of Adult Learning*. San Francisco, CA: Jossey-Bass.

Moch, M.K., and Bartunek, J.M. (1990) *Creating Alternative Realities at Work*. New York: Harper.

Moon, J. (1999) *Learning Journals: A Handbook for Academics, Students and Professional Development*. London: Kogan Page.

Morrison, B. and Lifford, R. (2001) 'How can action research apply to health services?', *Qualitative Health Research*, 11 (4): 436–49.

Nadler, D.A. (1977) *Feedback and Organization Development: Using Data-Based Methods*. Reading, MA: Addison-Wesley.

Nielsen, J.C.R. and Repstad, P. (1993) From nearness to distance – and back: Analyzing your own organization'. *Copenhagen Business School, Institute of Organizational and Industrial Sociology*, Papers in Organizations no. 14.

Pace, L.A. and Argona, D.R. (1991) 'Participatory action research: A view from Xerox', in W.W. Whyte (ed.), *Participatory Action Research*. Thousand Oaks, CA: Sage. pp. 56–69.

Pasmore, W.A. (2001) 'Action research in the workplace: The socio-technical perspective', in P. Reason and H. Bradbury (eds), *Handbook of Action Research*. London: Sage. pp. 38–47.

Pedler, M. (1996) *Action Learning for Managers*. London: Lemos and Crane.

Perry, C. and Zuber-Skerritt, O. (1994) 'Doctorates by action research for senior practising managers', *Management Learning*, 25 (2): 341–64.

Peter, J.P. and Olsen, J.C. (1983) 'Is marketing science?', *Journal of Marketing*, 47: 111–25.

Pettigrew, P. (2003) 'Power, conflicts and resolutions: A change agent's perspective on conducting action research within a multiorganizational partnership', *Systemic Practice and Action Research*, 16 (6): 375–91.

Potter, C., Morgan, P. and Thompson, A. (1994) 'Continuous quality improvement in an acute hospital', *International Journal of Health Care Quality Assurance*, 7 (1): 4–29.

Preskill, H. and Torres, R.T. (1999) *Evaluative Inquiry for Learning in Organizations*. Thousand Oaks, CA: Sage.

Punch, M. (1994) 'Politics and ethics in qualitative research', in N.K. Denzin and Y.S. Lincoln (eds), *Handbook of Qualitative Research*. Thousand Oaks, CA: Sage. pp. 83–97.

Putnam, R. (1991) 'Recipes and reflective learning', in D. Schon (ed.), *The Reflective Turn: Case Studies in and on Educational Practice*. New York: Teachers' College of Columbia Press. pp. 145–63.

Quick, J., Paulus, P., Whittington, J., Larey, T. and Nelson, D. (1996) *Management Development, Well-Being and Health*. Chichester: Wiley.

Quinlan, D.R. (1996) 'Towards a re-construction of a clinical psychologist and reflexive body of practice'. Unpublished PhD thesis, University of Bath.

Raelin, J.A. (1997) 'Action learning and action science: Are they different?' *Organizational Dynamics*, 26 (1): 21–34.

Raelin, J.A (1999) 'Preface'. *Management Learning*, 30 (2): 115-25.

Raelin, J.A. (2000) *Work-Based Learning: The New Frontier of Management Development*. Upper Saddle River, NJ: Prentice-Hall.

Ramirez, I. and Bartunek, J.M. (1989) 'The multiple realities and experience of internal organization development consultation in health care', *Journal of Organizational Change Management*, 2 (1): 40–56.

Rashford, N.S. and Coghlan, D. (1994) *The Dynamics of Organizational Levels: A Change Framework for Managers and Consultants*. Reading, MA: Addison-Wesley.

Reason, P. (1988) *Human Inquiry in Action*. London: Sage.

Reason, P (1999) 'Integrating action and reflection through cooperative inquiry', *Management Learning*, 30 (2): 207–26.

Reason. P. (2003) 'Choice and quality in action research practice', paper delivered at ALARPM 6th World Congress and PAR 10th World Congress, Pretoria, South Africa. http://www/bath.ac.uk/~mnspwr/Papers/Choice&Qualityin ActionResearchPractice.htm

Reason, P. and Bradbury, H. (2001) *Handbook of Action Research*. London: Sage.

Reason, P. and Marshall, J. (1987) 'Research as personal process', in D. Boud and V. Griffin (eds), *Appreciating Adult Learning*, London: Kogan Page. pp. 112–26.

Reason, P. and Marshall, J. (2001) 'On working with graduate research students', in P. Reason and H. Bradbury (eds), *Handbook of Action Research*. London: Sage. pp. 413–19.

Reason, P. and Torbert, W.R. (2001) 'The action turn: Toward a transformational social science', *Concepts and Transformation*, 6 (1): 1–37.

Revans, R. (1982) *The Origins and Growth of Action Learning*. Bromley: Chartwell-Bratt.

Revans, R. (1998) *ABC of Action Learning*. London: Lemos and Crane.

Riemer, J. (1977) 'Varieties of opportunistic research', *Urban Life*, 5 (4): 467–77.

Riordan, P. (1995) 'The philosophy of action science', *Journal of Managerial Psychology,* 10 (6): 6–13.

Ross, R. (1994) 'The ladder of inference', in P. Senge, C. Roberts, R. Ross, B. Smith and A. Kleiner (eds), *The Fifth Discipline Fieldbook*. London: Nicholas Brealey. pp. 242–6.

Ross, R. and Roberts, C. (1994) 'Balancing inquiry and advocacy', in P. Senge, C. Roberts, R. Ross, B. Smith and A. Kleiner (eds), *The Fifth Discipline Fieldbook*. London: Nicholas Brealey. pp. 253–9.

Roth, G. and Kleiner, A. (1998) 'Developing organizational memory through learning histories', *Organizational Dynamics*, 27 (3): 43–60.

Roth, G. and Kleiner, A. (2000) *Car Launch*. New York: Oxford University Press.

Roth, J., Sandberg, R. and Svensson, C. (2004) 'The dual role of the insider action researcher', in N. Adler, A.B (Rami) Shani and A. Styhre (eds), *Collaborative Research in Organizations*. Thousand Oaks, CA: Sage. pp. 117–34.

Rousseau, D. (1985) 'Issues in organizational research: Multi-level and cross-level perspectives', in L.L. Cummings, and B.M. Staw (eds), *Research in Organizational Behavior*, vol. 7. Greenwich, CT: JAI. pp. 1–37.

Rowan, J. (2000) 'Research ethics', *International Journal of Psychotherapy*, 5 (2): 103–10.

Rudolph, J., Taylor, S. and Foldy, E. (2001) 'Collaborative off-line reflection: A way to develop skill in action science and action inquiry', in P. Reason and H. Bradbury (eds), *Handbook of Action Research*. London: Sage. pp. 405–12.

Sagor, R. (1992) *How to Conduct Collaborative Action Research*. Alexandria, VA: Association for Supervision and Curriculum Development.

Schein, E.H. (1987) *The Clinical Perspective in Fieldwork*. Newbury Park, CA: Sage.

Schein, E.H. (1992) *Organizational Culture and Leadership*, 2nd edition. San Francisco, CA: Jossey-Bass.

Schein, E.H. (1996a) 'Three cultures of management', *Sloan Management Review*, 37 (3): 9–20.

Schein, E.H. (1996b). 'Kurt Lewin's change theory in the field and in the classroom: Notes toward a model of managed learning', *Systems Practice*, 9 (1): 27–48.

Schein, E.H. (1997) 'Organizational learning: What is new?', in M.A. Rahim, R.T. Golembiewski and L.E. Pate (eds), *Current Topics in Management,* vol. 2. Greenwich, CT: JAI. pp. 11–25.

Schein, E.H. (1999a) *Process Consultation Revisited: Building the Helping Relationship.* Reading, MA: Addison-Wesley.

Schein, E.H. (1999b) *The Corporate Culture Survival Guide*. San Francisco, CA: Jossey-Bass.

Schein, E.H. (2001) 'Clinical inquiry/research', in P. Reason and H. Bradbury (eds), *Handbook of Action Research*. London: Sage. pp. 228–37.

Schein, E.H. (2003) *DEC is Dead, Long Live DEC*. San Francisco, CA: Berrett-Koehler.

Schon, D. (1983) *The Reflective Practitioner*. New York: Basic Books.

Schon, D. (1987) *Educating the Reflective Practitioner*. San Francisco, CA: Jossey-Bass.

Schon, D. (1991) *The Reflective Turn: Case Studies in and on Educational Practice.* New York: Teachers' College of Columbia Press.

Seibert, K.W. and Daudelin, M.W. (1999) *The Role of Reflection in Managerial Learning*. Westport, CT: Quorum.

Selener, D. (1997) *Participatory Action Research and Social Change*. Ithaca, NY: Cornell Participatory Action Research Network.

Senge, P. (1990) *The Fifth Discipline*. New York: Doubleday.

Senge, P., Roberts, C., Ross, R., Smyth, B. and Kleiner, A. (1994) *The Fifth Discipline Fieldbook*. London: Nicholas Brealey.

Shani, A.B. (Rami) and Docherty, P. (2003) *Learning by Design*. Oxford: Blackwell.

Shani, A.B. (Rami) and Pasmore, W.A. (1985) 'Organization inquiry: Towards a new model of the action research process', in D.D. Warrick (ed.), *Contemporary*

Organization Development: Current Thinking and Applications. Glenview, IL: Scott, Foresman. pp. 438–48.

Shepard, H. (1997) 'Rules of thumb for change agents', in D. Van Eynde, J. Hoy and D.C. Van Eynde (eds), *Organization Development Classics*. San Francisco, CA: Jossey-Bass. pp. 181–90.

Simons, J. (2002) 'An action research study exploring how education may enhance pain management in children', *Nurse Education Today*, 22: 102–17.

Stringer, E.T. (1999) *Action Research: A Handbook for Practitioners*, 2nd edition, Thousand Oaks, CA: Sage.

Susman G. and Evered, R. (1978) 'An assessment of the scientific merits of action research', *Administrative Science Quarterly*, 23: 582–603.

Titchen, A. and Binnie, A. (1993) 'Research partnerships: Collaborative action research in nursing', *Journal of Advanced Nursing*, 18: 858–65.

Toulmin, S. and Gustavsen, B. (1996) *Beyond Theory: Changing Organizations through Participation*. Amsterdam: John Benjamins.

Torbert, W.R. (1987) *Managing the Corporate Dream*. Homewood, IL: Dow Jones-Irwin.

Torbert, W.R. (1989) 'Leading organizational transformation', in R. Woodman and W. Pasmore (eds), *Research in Organizational Change and Development*, vol. 3. Greenwich, CT: JAI. pp. 83–116

Torbert, W.R. (1991) *The Power of Balance*. Thousand Oaks, CA: Sage.

Torbert, W.R. (1999) 'The distinctive questions developmental action inquiry asks', *Management Learning*, 30 (2): 189–206.

Torbert, W.R. (2001) 'The practice of action inquiry', in P. Reason and H. Bradbury (eds), *Handbook of Action Research*. London: Sage. pp. 250–60.

Ury, W. (1991) *Getting Past No*. London: Business Books.

Walker, B. and Haslett, T. (2002) 'Action research in management–ethical dilemmas', *Systemic Practice and Action Research*, 15 (6): 523–33.

Waterman, H., Tillen, D., Dickson, R. and de Koning, K. (2001) 'Action research: A systematic review and guidance for assessment', *Health Technology Assessment,* 5 (23).

Webb, C. and Pontin, D. (1997) 'Evaluating the introduction of primary nursing: The use of a care plan audit', *Journal of Clinical Nursing*, 6: 395–401.

Weick, K. (1995) *Sensemaking in Organizations*. Thousand Oaks, CA: Sage.

Weisbord, M.R. (1988) 'Towards a new practice theory of OD: Notes on snap-shooting and moviemaking', in W.A. Pasmore and R.W Woodman (eds), *Research in Organizational Change and Development*, vol. 2. Greenwich, CT: JAI pp. 59–96.

Weisbord, M.R. (2004) *Productive Workplaces Revisited*, 2nd edition. San Francisco, CA: Jossey-Bass.

Wheelan, S.A. (1999) *Creating Effective Teams*. Thousand Oaks, CA: Sage.

Whyte, W.W. (1991) *Participatory Action Research*. Thousand Oaks, CA: Sage.

Williamson, G. and Prosser, S. (2002) 'Action research: Politics, ethics and participation', *Journal of Advanced Nursing*, 40: 587–93.

Winter, R. (1989) *Learning from Experience: Principle and Practice in Action Research*. London: Falmer Press.

Winter, R. and Munn-Giddings, C. (2001) *A Handbook of Action Research in Health and Social Care*. London: Routledge.

Young, M. (1991) *An Inside Job*. Oxford: Clarendon Press.

Zeichner, K. (2001) 'Educational action research', in P. Reason and H. Bradbury (eds), *Handbook of Action Research*. London: Sage. pp. 273–84.

Zuber-Skerritt, O. and Perry, C. (2002) 'Action research within organizations and university thesis writing', *The Learning Organization*, 9 (4): 171–9.

Appendix: Notes for Supervising Action Research

Action research is not an impersonal, external and solely intellectual exercise for the researcher. It is, rather, a complex range of personal and social processes, which consequently makes particular demands on those entrusted with the role of acting as supervisors (Reason and Marshall, 2001).

As action research involves the three domains of (a) the first-person practice of the individual researcher (b) the second-person practice of collaborative and political involvement with others, and (c) the third-person practice of the generation of usable knowledge, supervisor needs to attend to all three domains.

With respect to the individual researcher, the supervisor attends to the whole person – how that person's cognitive frameworks and emotional state are shaping action, how they are coping with the demands of the research work in conjunction with their personal lives.

With respect to collaborative and political involvement with others, supervisors facilitate reflection and feedback on how that researcher is engaging with others, and provide opportunities for role play rehearsal in anticipation of difficult situations where needed.

With respect to generating usable knowledge, this is familiar ground for supervisors and the role with which they are probably most comfortable. The adjustment supervisors need to make with respect to action research is that theory generation is primarily extrapolated from insider single-case situations, rather than from universal propositions.

In traditional research approaches there are typically clear stages, such as literature review, data collection, data analysis, and so on. Supervisors sign off on stages that are completed. For instance a supervisor can say that the literature review is adequate and effectively completed and that the research hypothesis is clearly formulated and then that the researcher can move on to the next stage. As action research is messy and involves concurrent iterative cycles of action and reflection supervising in terms of such stages is meaningless. Supervisors need to attend to the unfolding process in a mode that is akin to process consultation (Schein, 1999a).

Schein (1999a) provides a typology of inquiry interventions which is useful for academic supervisors of action research. He presents three general forms of inquiry:

1 *Pure Inquiry*: This is inquiry into the story. Supervisors may pose these sorts of questions: 'What is happening in the situation?'; 'Describe it'; 'Tell me more'.
2 *Exploratory-Diagnostic Inquiry*: This is inquiry into how the researcher is experiencing and understanding what is taking place in the research. Supervisors may pose questions which explore the researcher's (a) reasoning process – 'What do you think about that?'; (b) emotional responses – 'How do you feel about that?'; and (c) actions – 'Why do you do that?'
3 *Confrontive Inquiry*: This is inquiry which is being shaped by supervisors sharing their own responses and ideas that confront the researchers to consider alternative frames and actions. Such inquiry may focus on *process* – 'Could you . . .?' and on *content* – 'Have you considered . . .?'

As presented in Chapter 3, other typologies such as Torbert's four forms of speech or Argyris's hypotheses testing are appropriate.

Name Index

Subject Index